Joel N. Bloom
Director, Franklin Institute Science Museum
Cochairman

Earl A. Powell III
Director, Los Angeles County Museum of Art
Cochairman

Ellen Cochran Hicks
Project Director

Mary Ellen Munley
Research Coordinator

American Association of Museums

Washington, D.C.

Museums for a New Century

A Report of the Commission on Museums for a New Century

American Association of Museums
1055 Thomas Jefferson St., NW
Washington, D.C. 20007
(202) 338-5300
© 1984 by the American Association of Museums.
All rights reserved.
Published 1984
Printed in the United States of America
Library of Congress Catalog Card Number: 84-72051
ISBN 0-931201-08-X

Contents

List of Brief Reports

Foreword

Business has a stake in vital museums. They attract tourist dollars and contribute to urban revival. They help communities attract, hold and stimulate business talent. Our own experience at Philip Morris, as a sponsor of more than 100 cultural events and exhibitions over the last quarter century, has shown us clearly that business prospers where culture flourishes.

No longer elite preserves, museums now are part of a popular movement in which more Americans attend cultural events than professional sports. But museums can do more, and this report shows how. The American Association of Museums' Commission on Museums for a New Century has mapped what museums offer and has illuminated what they can become as laboratories for new technologies, forums for bold ideas and showplaces for artistic experimentation. The report makes a persuasive case that museums can supplement universities as centers of research and teaching.

Philip Morris is proud to join the Pew Memorial Trust as a major sponsor of the commission's work and is pleased to underwrite the publication and promotion of the commission's recommendations.

There is room for businesses large and small to become more involved with museums. The results can be almost as rewarding for everyone involved as a visit to a museum itself.

Hamish Maxwell

Chairman and Chief Executive Officer
Philip Morris Incorporated

Preface

When the Commission on Museums for a New Century began its work in 1982, it embarked for uncharted territory. Museums are devoted to investigating, recording and interpreting the world around us, yet ironically, there had never been a serious, analytical look at the rich and complex museum community, its past and present, let alone its future. Museums preserve the evidence of human existence and the natural world in order that future generations will know about their origins, but museum leaders had not begun to assess the part their institutions will play in the lives of those generations.

For museums in 1982, despite the effects of an uncertain economy, public visibility and popularity had never been greater. As the new century approached, leaders of the American Association of Museums saw that it was time for an examination of the major issues museums faced.

The commission was established to accomplish this formidable task: to study and clarify the role of museums in American society, their obligations to preserve and interpret our cultural and natural heritage, and their responsibilities to an ever-broadening audience. Craig C. Black, then president of the AAM, appointed a group of distinguished museum directors, trustees, and foundation and business leaders, and asked us to serve as cochairmen.

The commission has just one precedent. In 1969 the AAM published *America's Museums: The Belmont Report*, a document developed by the Committee on Museum Needs in response to a request by the federal government that the museum profession outline and justify its financial needs for the future. The Belmont Report, which laid the groundwork for our current system of federal support, represented a concerted effort by museum leaders to articulate their institutions' requirements for survival and growth.

Unlike Belmont, this commission has a broad charge. Our report is not a statement of specific needs or a "wish list" for the future but an assessment of American museums as a new century approaches. Our focus is on their purpose, why they are important to our culture and what they contribute to the quality of the human experience. We have certainly considered what museums need—and we will describe some of those needs—but we have emphasized what museums have and what they can give.

The commission had three objectives: to explore current social, economic, political and scientific trends that will affect the future of museums; to identify trends in the operations and needs of museums; and to describe the resulting opportunities and responsibilities facing the museum community.

Much has been accomplished since the commission first met. At open forums in New Orleans, San Francisco and Chicago, commission members and invited participants explored the issues that define a museum's relationship to its community. At four colloquiums, commission members discussed more specific issues with invited experts. The full commission convened four times to determine the scope of its work and settle on the process, to formulate the recommendations and to review the manuscript of this report.

Museums have many options, many paths to follow into what futurists call our "choiceful" future. The commission has tried to describe some of these options. Although this report is the most visible product of our work, we have accomplished much that will serve museums well in coming years. We have examined the social, economic, scientific and political trends that are shaping the society of the future and gained an understanding of the resulting prospects for museums. We have learned what museum professionals think about the state of museums today and their hopes for the future. We have heard about expectations as well as uncertainties, the urge to grow as well as the pressure to impose limits. The commission's work stimulated discussion of the philosophical foundations of museums, fundamental concerns so often pushed aside in the press of daily affairs.

The informed and interested public and professionals in related fields of work have told us of their perceptions of museums and the role they envision for museums in the future. In this exploration, we have expanded the community of museums to include people and institutions we should collaborate with in order to thrive and grow. This new network is still fragile, but it may prove to be one of the most valuable results of our work. It includes those who met with us in open forums and colloquiums, representatives of organizations involved in future planning and people the staff consulted in its research. Many of these people were prompted to think seriously about the nature of museums for the first time. In the process, they developed a new interest in the role of museums in society and a continuing interest in working with the museum community.

It was a challenging task to make judgments about the issues we would address in depth. Writing for such a diverse audience is difficult at best, so some readers undoubtedly will wish we had considered certain issues more fully. We chose the focus for this report in the interest of the museum community as a whole and with the hope of opening new ideas to discussion.

The report has three elements: the narrative, the commission's recommendations and brief reports accompanying the text. Our 16 recommendations, which appear throughout the text but are printed together at the end of chapter 1, are not intended to be isolated from the context of the full report or construed as presented in order of priority. They are suggestions for action or statements of the commission's collective opinion on the issues raised in this report. The brief reports, which are based on information acquired in the commission's research, illustrate the abundance of excellent programs carried out by museums, groups of museums and professional organizations. Some amplify the narrative; others describe particular programs that put the commission's ideas and recommendations into action.

The generosity of a number of foundations, corporations and museums made possible the work of the Commission on Museums for a New Century. The Pew Memorial Trust provided major support for the first phase—the meetings and staff research that led the commission to the conclusions in this report. Robert I. Smith, president of the Glenmede Trust Company, which administers the trust, was enthusiastic from the start about what the commission could do for museums in America. Smith and his staff were willing to take a risk on a project unlike any other undertaken by the museum community, and we are extremely grateful for this expression of confidence.

Philip Morris Incorporated provided major support for the second phase of the project—the writing and publication of the commission report and, through an in-kind contribution, publicity and promotion efforts. Additional support came from the Charles Ulrick and Josephine Bay Foundation, the J. Paul Getty Trust and the Samuel H. Kress Foundation. The commission also received grants and contributions from AT&T Foundation, the Equitable Life Assurance Society of the United States, the Mobil Foundation, the Smithsonian Institution's National Museum of Natural History, the Square D Foundation, the Louisiana State Museum Foundation, the Missouri Botanical Garden, the Natural History Museum of Los Angeles County, the American Express Foundation and the AAM Education Committee.

Finally, we commend the American Association of Museums—particularly its director, Lawrence L. Reger, and its current and immediate past presidents, Thomas W. Leavitt and Craig C. Black— for pursuing this important project on behalf of America's museums.

We pay special tribute here to three commission members whose contributions to our work were at first profoundly felt and then sorely missed. Mamie Phipps Clark (1918–83) was devoted throughout her life to the education and emotional well-being of black children and committed to museums as an essential part of the human experience. As chairman of the National Endowment for the Arts and a special friend of museums, Nancy Hanks (1927–83) brought artists and cultural institutions to a vibrant place at the center of our nation's life. William G. Swartchild (1907–84), an active, forward-thinking trustee and a dedicated participant in the affairs of the museum community, epitomized the qualities of a museum leader.

We acknowledge, too, the work of the commission's drafting committee. Kenneth Starr chaired the committee with skill and wisdom. The other members—Craig C. Black, Edmund Barry Gaither, Thomas W. Leavitt, Helmuth J. Naumer and Peter H. Raven—spent considerable time with us and the staff in a thorough review of the manuscript in every stage of its development.

Research, writing and support for all the commission's activities were conducted by the commission's staff under the direction of Ellen Cochran Hicks, who synthesized the commission's discussions into the report we offer here. Mary Ellen Munley guided the research efforts for the commission. Carolee Belkin Walker and her predecessor Sally Jordalen provided research and administrative assistance. The manuscript was edited by Ann Hofstra Grogg.

The commission process has been exciting, instructive, occasionally frustrating, rich in information and ideas. We have confirmed our sense that museums admirably fulfill their mission and purpose and strengthened our belief that the health of any institution or profession depends on a clear, unified sense of purpose and the capacity to think ahead. The process is far from finished, however. The publication of this report should mark the beginning of a sustained effort by the museum community to know its potential, to know the forces shaping the society museums serve and to use that knowledge in forging a productive role for museums in the world of the 21st century.

The future holds both challenges and vexing problems for museums. At one commission colloquium, a social scientist commented on the erosion of public confidence in the nation's institutions. Museums, he said, are the exception. Given this public confidence, and the increasing evidence of the value of museums to our lives, society will need museums more in the future than ever before.

"To clarify an ever-changing present and to inform the future with wisdom"—this message, inscribed near the entrance to Dumbarton Oaks in Washington, D.C., is an apt description of the commission's work. If we have met this ambitious challenge, we have done our work well. Now the task belongs to the museum community and to all those who want the future of museums to be even richer than the past. Our museums reflect what we are and what we have been. We all have a stake in what they will be.

Joel N. Bloom
Earl A. Powell III

Washington, D.C.
July 1984

Joel N. Bloom (cochairman), Director
Franklin Institute Science Museum
Philadelphia, Pa.

Earl A. Powell III (cochairman), Director
Los Angeles County Museum of Art
Los Angeles, Calif.

George H. J. Abrams, Director
Seneca-Iroquois National Museum
Salamanca, N.Y.

Craig C. Black, Director
Natural History Museum of Los Angeles County
Los Angeles, Calif.

Mamie Phipps Clark (deceased), President
Museums Collaborative, Inc.
New York, N.Y.

Mildred S. Compton, Director Emeritus
Children's Museum
Indianapolis, Ind.

William G. Conway, Director
New York Zoological Society
New York, N.Y.

George Ewing, Former Cultural Affairs Officer
State of New Mexico
Santa Fe, N.M.

Richard Fiske, Director
National Museum of Natural History
Smithsonian Institution, Washington, D.C.

Edmund Barry Gaither, Director
Museum of the National Center of Afro-American
 Artists
Boston, Mass.

Nancy Hanks (deceased), Former Chairman
National Endowment for the Arts
Washington, D.C.

F. Wayne King, Director
Florida State Museum, University of Florida
Gainesville, Fla.

Thomas W. Leavitt, Director
Herbert F. Johnson Museum of Art
Cornell University, Ithaca, N.Y.

Richard W. Lyman, President
Rockefeller Foundation
New York, N.Y.

Robert R. Macdonald, Director
Louisiana State Museum
New Orleans, La.

Jan Keene Muhlert, Director
Amon Carter Museum of Art
Fort Worth, Tex.

Franklin D. Murphy, Chairman
Executive Committee, Times-Mirror Company
Los Angeles, Calif.

Helmuth J. Naumer, Executive Director
San Antonio Museum Association
San Antonio, Tex.

Richard E. Oldenburg, Director
Museum of Modern Art
New York, N.Y.

Eldridge H. Pendleton, Director of Collections
 and Programs
Old York Historical Society
York, Maine

Peter H. Raven, Director
Missouri Botanical Garden
St. Louis, Mo.

Harold K. Skramstad, Jr., President
Edison Institute at Henry Ford Museum and
 Greenfield Village
Dearborn, Mich.

Kenneth Starr, Director
Milwaukee Public Museum
Milwaukee, Wis.

William G. Swartchild, Jr. (deceased), Trustee
Field Museum of Natural History
Chicago, Ill.

Ex-Officio Members

Lawrence L. Reger, Director
American Association of Museums

Peter N. Kyros, Jr., Legislative Counsel
American Association of Museums

Commission Staff

Ellen Cochran Hicks, Project Director
Mary Ellen Munley, Research Coordinator
Carolee Belkin Walker, Research Assistant

Museums for a New Century

1 The Growing Museum Movement

During one of the commission's open forums, we were reminded of Aristotle's belief that men and women come together in cities in order to become more human. "Certainly," we were told, "men and women come into museums in some ways to become more human and to discover . . . that collective experience charged with moral energy is still alive and well in America." The act of contributing to the richness of the collective human experience is at the very heart of what museums are all about. By helping us summon our natural capacities for empathy, for vicarious experience, for intellectual growth, museums summon the humanity in us.

Through their collections and their programs, museums offer rich encounters with reality, with the past, with what exists now and with what is possible. They stimulate curiosity, give pleasure, increase knowledge. Museums acquaint us with the unfamiliar, coaxing us beyond the safety of what we already know. And they impart a freshness to the familiar, disclosing miracles in what we have long taken for granted. Museums are gathering places, places of discovery, places to find quiet, to contemplate and to be inspired. They are our collective memory, our chronicle of human creativity, our window on the natural and physical world.

Museums in this country are individually magnificent, from the large and encyclopedic institutions to the small and jewel-like collections, from new neighborhood museums to institutions a century old, from art galleries, to botanical gardens, to historic sites, to science-technology centers to zoos. Together, museums are even more magnificent. Their collective significance to American life, their aggregate value, makes museums a national resource. They are the stewards of this country's common wealth—a wealth of spirit, of substance, of cultural abundance.

American museums today are enormously popular places. There are nearly 5,000 of them, in all regions of the country, in communities of all sizes. Our nation's museums have a long tradition of scholarship, education and public service. Their contributions to our intellectual and cultural life, their capacity for encouraging inquiry and vision, make them cornerstones of a democratic society. Millions of people visit museums each year, seeking knowledge, enjoyment and a greater understanding of other peoples, other places, other times. Museums help make their communities pleasing to live in and visit, too; as cultural amenities, they help attract business investment and the tourist dollar.

Beyond the direct significance of museums to their communities and their visitors is the constellation of values museums represent. The commitment to preserving, cherishing and learning from the artifacts and customs of our heritage—a commitment museums were the first to make—is permeating American life. There is a new enthusiasm for collecting, for acquiring objects that have personal meaning or represent disappearing traditions of craftsmanship. On a larger scale, the values museums espouse launched the historic preservation movement and helped fuel the growing pride in community and ethnic history.

Museums represent certainty in uncertain times. As contemporary life grows more impersonal, people need to be reminded that there is a continuity to human existence and the natural and physical world, and they need a way to connect their own experience to what is known about

The Expanding Museum Universe

From the first great surge in museum founding in the late 1800s, the American museum universe has been expanding in both scope and size. The most recent surge occurred around the Bicentennial, when many communities were inspired to explore their local identities through the establishment of museums. In addition, all kinds of collection-oriented cultural and scientific institutions are now perceiving themselves as museums. The museum universe now includes traditional art, history and science museums as well as art and science centers, children's museums, zoos, botanical gardens and aquariums.

Changing times and changing perceptions result in new museums. With increased recognition of our country's diverse cultures, some outstanding ethnic and minority museums have been established. Institutions such as the Mexican Museum in San Francisco, the Museum of American Jewish History in Philadelphia, the Museum of the National Center of Afro-American Artists in Boston and the Seneca-Iroquois National Museum in Salamanca, New York, have now joined the museum domain. Together they tell the story of our nation's cultural pluralism.

Technological advances and new appreciation for the daily life of common people also create a need for new museums. Radio and television—both 20th-century phenomena—are the focus of the collections and research at the Museum of Broadcasting, which opened in New York City in 1976. Responding to another new technology, the Computer Museum opened in Boston in June 1983. With a collection of old and not-so-old calculators, computers and parts of computers, it is dedicated to the preservation of computing history. The Center for Creative Photography in Tucson, Arizona, recognizes photography as both documentary evidence and art form, and the Craft and Folk Art Museum in Los Angeles is one of several dozen museums now dedicated to the collection, research and exhibition of American crafts—objects only recently appreciated for their sociological significance and their beauty.

Museums in this country endeavor to reflect the whole of human experience. As that experience expands, so does the museum universe. Presently museums are being planned on the topics of women artists and the Holocaust. Even now, science and industry and everyday people are creating the museum collections of the future. The most popular museum in the world—the Smithsonian's National Air and Space Museum—opened less than a decade ago and could scarcely have been imagined two decades before that.

the past and the present. It could be said that our times are creating a museum movement.

During the course of our work for the commission, we found evidence of this growing museum movement. We heard expressions of respect for museums and admiration for the museum community's eagerness to prepare for the future. We perceived considerable confidence in the constant, enduring and familiar characteristics of museums. From city planner Alan Jacobs, who talked of his "incredible and growing joy" in going to museums, to newspaper columnist Kevin Starr, who said museums are places where "people can come and feel that what is done is important and possessed of authority," the people who participated in the commission process reaffirmed that museums—and the values they represent—are the touchstones our society needs now and for the future.

It is precisely this public confidence that offers museums a significant challenge: how to retain their permanence and authority while embracing a larger public role and responding to new social responsibilities. It is important to remember that American museums have always been engaged in a process of democratization. Unlike their European counterparts, which were usually founded to house the great collections of the nobility, American museums evolved in a tradition befitting a democratic society. Nathaniel Burt describes it this way:

> The American museum was and is an idea. The European museum was a fact. Almost without exception the European museum was first a collection. With few exceptions most American museums were first an ideal. . . . Almost without exception the larger American museums began with a deliberate appeal to the public. Most of the earlier European museums remained semi-exclusive cabinets of curiosities visible only to a few. The American museum began, and has remained, wide open.

Although American museums owe a great deal to the beneficence of collectors and patrons, many of them indeed grew out of the deliberate desire to diffuse useful knowledge, to refine public taste, to take responsibility for what Benjamin Ives Gilman called "forwarding the life of the imagination." Early atheneums assembled collections for scientific and literary study. Art museums were founded with the idea that the public should enjoy great art. A strong pride in the new nation gave rise to the preservation of historic sites.

Museums have a strong and credible position as institutions in society today because they have always assumed a public dimension. The charters of museums founded in the 19th century embraced the Victorian impulse toward social reform. In the 1930s and 1940s museums sought to stress their educational function. The fervent idealism of the 1960s prompted museums even further toward social consciousness.

Perhaps the largest steps in the democratization of museums in the United States have been taken in the last 15 years. In the turbulence of the late 1960s and early 1970s, museums were perceived as ivory towers outside the mainstream of society. Their traditional authority was challenged, their relevance to society questioned. In the struggle to respond, museums reaffirmed their commitment to a public role. They reached out into the community, initiating programs for senior citizens, minorities, the handicapped and others who traditionally had felt excluded. The community of museums itself expanded to include new institutions addressing interests and heritages not adequately represented in existing institutions. Both physically and intellectually, museums became more accessible to more people.

At the same time, museums, along with other institutions in the nonprofit sector, recognized their close relationship to the rest of society and accepted a fuller sense of accountability for their actions. "The texture of American life," Stephen E. Weil has observed, "is thickening. No matter how special we may feel, [museums] are an inextricable part of the American community, and its future will be ours. As its life becomes more complex, so will ours."

In the course of this "thickening," museums have taken more seriously their obligations as public trusts. They have established both institutional and individual standards of quality and ethics. A broad-based, public-private system of financial support has developed, with government, business, foundations, individuals and museums themselves all sharing the responsibility. What has evolved in the past 15 years is, in short, a much higher degree of self-consciousness. Museums are now more deeply aware of their public obligations and their integral role in our nation's social and cultural life.

Museums also see more clearly their connection to one another. There is an emerging sense of

The Economic Impact of Museums

Economic impact studies are *pro forma* in the 1980s, and the arts have joined the bandwagon. In 1981 the National Endowment for the Arts published a pioneering report on the economic impact of arts and cultural institutions. Forty-nine institutions in six cities across the country reported a total direct economic impact of more than $68 million for the year 1979. Overall, 85 percent of total operating expenditures of the arts organizations were spent in local communities for goods, services and wages. In addition, local visitors and tourists at cultural institutions spent nearly $25 million on ancillary activities. The indirect economic impact (in local real estate, sales, income, lodging, gasoline and parking taxes) was more than $237 million. It is clear that culture pays!

A separate group of three studies in six New England states conducted by the New England Foundation for the Arts shows an aggregate economic impact from cultural organizations of $1.5 billion, confirming the critical role of the arts in the economy of the region. In 1978, 2,830 cultural organizations in New England spent $213 million, for a total economic impact of $560 million in New England and $75 million in the rest of the United States. They provided 42,849 jobs and returned $10 million in federal income taxes and $2.7 million in state taxes. In 1979, audiences attending New England visual and performing arts events spent an additional $142.3 million over and above admission costs, for a total economic impact of $352.7 million. In the state of Connecticut, for example, visual arts organizations such as the Wadsworth Atheneum in Hartford spent more than $5 million, provided 659 jobs and returned $236,754 in federal and state taxes in a single year.

New museums are often central to community economic development. The opening of the new Charles Shipman Payson Building of the Portland Museum of Art in May 1983 made an important economic and psychological impact on the small municipality of Portland, Maine (population 61,000). Even before the museum opened, buildings in the adjacent Congress Square area benefited from upgraded first-floor retail space, new retail activity, the conversion of an old building into apartments and the renovation of a hotel. Once opened, the new building brought an additional 3,000 people into the area every week, and, aside from visiting the museum, these people stopped at neighboring restaurants and shops. The direct and indirect economic impact of the museum's new construction was estimated at $28 million by the Center for Research and Advanced Study at the University of Southern Maine. According to its report, during 1984—the first year of the new building's operation—the museum's projected annual operating expenditures of about $1 million would produce a total economic impact of approximately $2.3 million.

In addition to the dollar figures cited by economic impact studies, museums make other economic contributions. A study conducted for the U.S. Congress on the attractiveness of cities for prospective businesses found that quality of life was more important to expanding and relocating firms than were business-related factors like tax rates and labor costs. More than 1,200 respondents in 10 American cities reported that the greatest disparity perceived among cities was in quality of life characteristics, and of seven variables viewed as most important, two were the availability of cultural attractions and adequate public facilities such as parks and libraries.

One of the study's conclusions was that improving a city's quality of life can have a significant influence on the decisions firms make regarding location and work force changes. This mounting evidence invalidates the image of nonprofit cultural organizations as economic losers and a drain on local resources. The question is not what the economy can do for the arts, but what the arts can do for the economy.

community among museums, a kind of internal democratization, that defies the arguments of those who thought museums were too disparate to speak a common language. There *are* differences among museums—some of them superficial, some fundamental—but the differences seem to make the community thrive. The American museum universe has been expanding in both scope and size since the 19th century and will likely continue to grow as the times demand. In fact, we contend that the healthy future of this country's museums depends on the recognition that each institution lends its own variation to the objectives all museums share. It may be difficult to imagine the similarities among such institutions as the Metropolitan Museum of Art, the Chesapeake Bay Maritime Museum, the Indianapolis Children's Museum, the Adler Planetarium, the San Diego Zoo and Colonial Williamsburg. But all have a legitimate place in the museum domain through their dedication to real things and the ideas those things embody.

The act of collecting and preserving objects is at the center of the museum domain. Just as important is the use of collections to advance knowledge and understanding, and thus it is through research, education and exhibition that museums make their collections available. The balance among these activities differs from museum to museum. Some museums use their collections primarily for research, while others mount ambitious exhibition programs. The larger museums do all these things, serving as centers of excellence in the intellectual and cultural life of this country as well as in the museum community. Other museums engage in all these activities, but with fewer resources and less ambitious objectives. Still others focus on one activity more than others—the art center that concentrates on exhibitions, for example. But all museums share their dedication to the object as tangible evidence of our artistic, cultural, natural and scientific heritage. What we have in the community of museums is a vibrant pluralism that allows differences to flourish while, faithful to the meaning of "community," we work together in a shared service toward shared goals and the worthy stewardship of our nation's common wealth.

This report is for all who care about museums and the future of their contribution to the collective human experience. Our rapidly changing society will look to museums even more in the years to come. How well museums respond depends on

Small Museums

Small is beautiful, and that's as true in the museum community as elsewhere. Small museums are not just lesser versions of large institutions. They are museums that make a distinctive contribution to their communities and the museum domain generally, for each does something special that no other institution can.

One of the staunchest supporters of small museums is Gerald George, director of the American Association for State and Local History in Nashville, Tennessee. AASLH represents the interests of museums and historic properties dedicated to local community history, and as such it looks out for the concerns of a very important segment of the museum domain. George likes to repeat an inscription from a London subway poster: "Local museums are treasure houses where unlikely objects—curious, ingenious, comic, even beautiful—lie stranded for our gaze. They indicate local pride and a sense of identity. More vividly evocative of the everyday past than our grander institutions, they deserve and reward our notice."

The hidden treasures of small museums are the Wedgwoods found in the decorative arts collection at the Thomas County Historical Society in Colby, Kansas, and a folk artist's rendering of four centuries of island life displayed at the Museum of Coastal History in St. Simons Island, Georgia. They reach as far as the Alaska State Museum in Juneau, where native culture is preserved through artifacts of aboriginal Alaskans. Half a continent away visitors with just a day to spend in Tucson can capture the flavor of the area by walking through a convincing coal mine and a desert landscape—both the exhibits of local museums. Small museums tell important stories about regional heritages and the life of the common people; they provide a sense of belonging and place.

The best among the small museums are those that build on the particular contribution they alone can make to their communities. The Canal Museum in Syracuse, New York, for instance, recently refined its purpose. In the past it had attempted to collect artifacts related to canals all over the world, but its location and limited resources made that impossible. With a new and stronger regional focus, the museum now plays a significant educational role in the community, teaching local history as part of the fourth-grade social studies curriculum.

Of course, some small museums get larger as they get better. Such is the case of the Littleton Historical Museum in Littleton, Colorado. Like many small museums, it was established by enthusiastic local people who had been collecting historical materials for years. In 1970, supporters struck a deal with the city government—if they could raise enough money to start a museum, the city would pay for continued operations. Now, 14 years later, the museum has an annual budget of about $400,000 and is totally supported by the 35,000 residents of Littleton.

Key to the success of this, and any, local museum, is a close tie to the community. Robert McQuarie, director of the Littleton Museum, explains, "We don't say there is a museum and a city—we are as much a part of the city as the firehouse."

their ability to sustain their current momentum. Given the pervasiveness of the values they stand for, their strong ties to the rest of society and their growing sense of common identity, museums are in an excellent position to become their own most forceful advocates, to make their significance both profoundly felt and highly esteemed. The collective human experience, now more than ever, needs the enrichment museums can offer.

The Shape of the Future

The close of a century, the end of a millennium, 1984—all are symbolically appropriate times to take stock, review the past, consider the future. As the next century draws closer, we will enter a new, postindustrial era in which our machine-oriented system gives way to an idea- and information-centered system. We will be presented with a new range of choices about the ethical and qualitative character of our lives. Today we have one foot in the past, while the other tests the future. We know how much social and technological change has already altered our lives, and we know we must monitor it carefully if we are to retain our individualism. We cannot wait for the future to happen; we must embrace it and participate actively in its creation.

We are already experiencing many of the conditions that will shape the 21st century: massive geopolitical shifts, changes in the distribution of material wealth, a technological revolution, demographic change, dramatic assaults on the ecosystem, rising levels of education, a transition in the developed world to an economy based on information and the provision of services. The ramifications of natural phenomena and human actions are global in scale, leaving relatively little of the earth unaffected, and the dimension of change will continue to accelerate.

More than half the human beings ever born are alive today. Within a few years, five billion people will share this planet, and by the end of the century, more than six billion. At that time only 20 percent of the world's population will live in what we now consider the developed world—the United States, Canada, Europe, the Soviet Union, Japan, Australia and New Zealand.

This fraction of the world's people now controls more than three-quarters of the world's wealth and consumes 85 percent of its resources. In the tropics, on the other hand, a third of the people are unable to obtain enough food for themselves and their families to avoid starvation.

The effects of such alarming imbalances impose new challenges for all social institutions in the developed world, including museums. On an international scale, museums foster the vital realization that we are citizens of a single planet in which the need for cooperation grows stronger every year. At the same time, museums can help preserve the diversity of human culture—a diversity rapidly disappearing.

Museums have another significant responsibility to educate people about the ability of our planet to sustain life. We live in an age in which plants and animals are becoming extinct at the most rapid rate in 65 million years. What this means is that up to one-sixth or more of the forms of life on earth may disappear forever during our lifetimes—a truly enormous change on a planetary scale, and one that may well seriously limit human potential in the future.

At the same time, our technological options are proliferating. The unprecedented scientific advances of the last 50 years and their accompanying applications have irrevocably altered our relationship to each other and our world. Many ravaging diseases are only history to us; the global attack on smallpox, for example, has completely eliminated it as a danger to human life, and antibiotics now effectively control tuberculosis and many other life-threatening diseases. We tinker with our hearts as if they were automobile engines, scan our bodies electronically and use laser surgery to correct problems we find. In the palms of our hands we hold devices that can outperform the room-sized computers of the early 1960s. Our nuclear capabilities make it possible for us to destroy virtually every living thing on earth. We know much about the workings of the universe, but we also have the ability to manipulate it. Both the possibilities and the dangers are greater than ever before.

Museums can help bring about what futurists call a "choiceful future," because they deal with both the possibilities and the dangers. Zoos and botanical gardens must find better ways to preserve and perpetuate their living collections, for as habitats disappear, some kinds of plants and animals will exist only in these institutions. Science museums and science-technology centers have a public obligation to explain research develop-

ments and technological innovation and draw attention to the ethical questions they raise. And clearly, museums of art and history must be firmly committed to preserving the expressions of human creativity and the material evidence of an existence that is so profoundly affected by the global scale of change today.

Perhaps the only statement we can make with complete certainty about the next century is that it is not likely to be tranquil. It will not be a time for "business as usual," for museums, for anyone. There will be great stress, tremendous problems and a pressing need for high creativity. For museums, the trusted guardians of the objects of our heritage, the challenge will be to achieve the highest form of public service.

Museums and the Forces of Change

The commission set out to examine the state of American museums at the close of this century. As we looked at the social, economic, scientific and political trends shaping society today, we paid careful attention to those we believe should be of special importance to museums. Studying the future is, we discovered, something of a trend itself. Futures research is a serious, useful process that does not attempt to approach prediction but to encourage careful thought about the possibilities we might find ahead, with "choice" and "options" the operative words. Business, government, education—all have adopted methods of futures research and incorporated them into their own planning.

In considering museums, we looked at economic and demographic trends; changes in the family, the workplace and education; current transitions in values and lifestyles and new directions in science and technology. Having considered—from our future-oriented vantage point—the context in which museums function, we can attest to the value of the exercise, and we commend it to individual museums.

We have identified four forces of change in society today that will have significant implications for museums. Just as these forces will influence the future of museums, so have they guided this commission in its work and provided the foundation for our conclusions and recommendations.

Forces of Change

A Proliferation of Voices

- Americans are moving toward an ethic of private commitment, founded on a giving-getting compact. In the public arena, they are demanding that social responsibility be demonstrated.
- Public participation in institutional decision making is growing.
- American society is decentralizing. The power, resources and initiatives for dealing with crises are coming from the bottom up. Regional coalitions are forming and increasing in importance.
- Networks, collaborations and cooperative systems for sharing are challenging hierarchical and competitive systems.
- Economic strain and hard times are expected to set the tone for the 1980s and the years beyond. Creative management, foresight and careful long-term economic planning will be prerequisites for survival.
- Dichotomies are disappearing. People have begun to demand—and are getting—a multitude of choices.
- Americans are in the midst of a transition in values. They are defining self-fulfillment in new ways, by demanding meaningful work and reexamining major social institutions such as marriage, the family and education.

Coming to Terms with Cultural Pluralism

- Except for large coastal cities such as New York, San Francisco and Miami, new immigrants no longer congregate in city centers. More often they choose to live in suburbs or small communities in the country's vast interior. There are now as many immigrants living in the suburbs as in the city centers.
- Twenty-five percent of the annual increase in population in this country is due to immigration. One million people immigrate to the United States each year. Forty percent are hispanics; another 40 percent are Asians.
- More than half of the U.S. population growth in the next two decades will come from minorities. By 2000, 20 percent of the U.S. population will be black or hispanic.
- Hispanics are the fastest growing minority; by 2000 hispanics will represent 10.9 percent of the total population—an increase from 18 million to 26 million people. Sixty percent of the hispanic population lives in California, Texas and New York.
- The proportion of Americans who are white and of European ancestry— the nation's basic ethnic stock since colonial days— will decline at an accelerating rate in the next two decades. By 2000, for example, the number of Asians in the population will rise at least 90 percent, from close to 4 million today to nearly 8 million.
- With the increased awareness of the multiplicity of cultures residing in the United States, there is a pressing need for a spirit of global community that respects ethnic and cultural differences.

A Proliferation of Voices

The first force of change concerns the way decisions are made. Quite simply, the way things get done is changing. Traditional hierarchical structures are being modified to accommodate, and in fact encourage, wider participation in the processes by which authority is vested and decisions are made. There is growing evidence of participatory decision making in the emergence of special-interest politics, the formation of new coalitions and networks to accomplish goals, the move toward new management styles, and challenges to the authority of large institutions, established professions and influential individuals. There are more voices involved in making decisions that affect individuals, segments of society and society as a whole. Consequently, both individuals and institutions face a wide array of options. Institutions that traditionally hold authority, too, are being compelled to examine and even modify their role in the larger society.

Participatory modes of decision making will have both internal and external implications for museums. Internally, new styles of management may affect governance and leadership. Collaborative, nonhierarchical approaches may alter internal institutional structures. Externally, museums will have to continue to explore possibilities for collaboration with other museums and cultural and community organizations. As a group with special interests of its own, the museum community needs to ensure that its base of support is broad and firm, and its unified voice clear, in order to secure an effective place in the changing political process.

Coming to Terms with Cultural Pluralism

The second major force of change we believe to have implications for museums is our society's evolving sense of its own pluralism. Our population has always been culturally and ethnically diverse, but that diversity has not always been accepted as a good thing. In recent years, however, cultural and ethnic heritages have been recognized as a distinctive element of the American character.

Yet we continue to be troubled by a fragmentation in our society. Assimilation as a national goal has been abandoned, and socioeconomic, racial and sexual inequality persists. In addition to the racial and ethnic diversity with which we are beginning to come to terms, we are asked to accept new lifestyles and different value systems.

There is uncertainty, too, in attitudes toward changing family structures, new sex roles, new models for the structure of the workplace. We are also in the midst of marked shifts in the median age, birth rate and geographic concentrations of population and wealth. New centers of political and economic power are forming in the process.

When it comes to preserving cultural pluralism, museums have an important role to play. They represent cultural diversity in their collections and their exhibitions. The museum community—within its own institutional makeup—exemplifies our cultural pluralism. Institutions dedicated to fostering and preserving particular ethnic heritages will be increasingly important in helping Americans understand their historical experience from different perspectives. But museums are in an uncomfortably contradictory situation in that their celebration of pluralism does not always extend to their internal hierarchies. Their staffs and boards generally do not represent the full diversity of our society. This challenge of cultural pluralism to museums is immediate and especially complex. We will address it more directly in chapter 4.

An Upheaval in Education

The condition of this country's educational system has given rise to the third force of change in which museums have a stake. During 1982 and 1983 there were calls for more rigorous standards in curriculum content, teacher preparation and the measurement of achievement. In *A Nation at Risk*, the National Commission on Excellence in Education chronicled the inadequacies of the nation's schools and urged widespread reform. *High School*, a report from the Carnegie Foundation for the Advancement of Teaching, demanded improvements in the nation's secondary schools. In *Educating Americans for the 21st Century*, a special commission of the National Science Board decried the state of education in science, mathematics and technology, calling for widespread, fundamental change and a greater role for museums and other institutions of informal learning.

On the positive side, informal, voluntary education is gaining credibility as more and more people—particularly adults—look for ways to im-

An Upheaval in Education

- Sixty-six percent of Americans hold high school diplomas; 16 percent have college degrees.
- Fifty percent of all children between 3 and 5 years old were enrolled in preschool programs in 1978.
- With the declining birthrate, school enrollment is expected to drop as much as 25 percent in the 1980s. In addition, because of a reduced college-age population and high tuition costs, 25 percent of all residential liberal arts colleges will close by the year 2000.
- Adult participation in educational programs has increased significantly. Adult education is the fastest-growing type of education today, and education is the most common adult discretionary time activity outside of the home.
- Thirty-five percent of all students enrolled in higher education are more than 24 years old; 70 percent of those are part-time students.
- Midcareer training programs have increased in popularity.
- Education is regarded as one of many commodities competing for the consumer dollar. Educational establishments are increasingly asked to deliver custom-tailored products on demand. They are asked to be accountable and to revise programs to meet the needs of consumers.

Wiring in to the Information Age

- Basic or applied knowledge and information will be our most important product in the coming decades.
- Science, as the source of knowledge and value systems, will be the central drive in American society.
- Industry is being urged to move as rapidly as possible to exploit the productive efficiency and powerful capacity of information and communication technologies.
- The capacity of a computer memory chip has increased approximately 64 times since 1971.
- By 1990, 30 million home computers will have been sold.
- Fifty percent of all jobs are related to the handling of information.
- Some members of our society are ill equipped to benefit from the coming of the information age.
- Some experts predict that high technology brings a "high-touch" reaction—an increasing need for individual choice and human interaction and for the serious consideration of ethical questions surrounding the use of technology. Many point to the health profession, where the introduction of life-support systems raised debate about their use and the right of patients to control their lives and deaths.

prove their skills, increase their personal knowledge or simply enjoy their more abundant leisure. The changing demographic characteristics of the population—an older population as the baby boom generation moves through adulthood, speculation about a smaller baby boom that will reverse the trend of declining school enrollments—will make education a focus for debate for decades to come.

In a society that puts such heavy emphasis on education and has such high expectations for its schools, it is not surprising that tumult and cries for reform so frequently prevail. The real strengths in the system may well be obscured now by attempts to make schools serve too great a variety of social needs. As it reaches to the heart of the problem, the current reform movement forces a reassessment of the realistic limits of formal education. In museums, too, the meaning of the learning experience, the relation of museums to schools and the mechanism for education in the museum setting are all worth careful attention. For that reason, we have devoted a full chapter of this report to the museum learning experience.

Wiring in to the Information Age

The phenomenal revolution in communication and information technology is the fourth force of change that will have serious implications for museums in the future. We live in a "wired society," in which television and the microchip alone have made the experience of our generation profoundly different. Only 15 years ago we were amazed to sit in front of our televisions and see men walk on the moon. Today we accept the instant connection to distant events as commonplace. Now entering its fifth generation, the computer has evolved from a cumbersome giant that could do complex mathematics to a portable machine that can manage a whole realm of information and is quickly becoming an accepted part of our daily lives. The intensified competition for the home computer market during the past few years is an indication that the computer soon will be, like the television set, a piece of household furniture.

Museums can both affect and be affected by the electronic age. Information management technology, too, could very well revolutionize museum operations, especially in collections management and public programs. In the way they choose to use communications technology in their exhibition halls and educational activities, however, museums can have a civilizing, humanizing influence on a population that may need a respite from the "high-tech" era. There could be wider access to museums through new forms of communication, not replacing the museum experience but giving more people the incentive to enjoy museums at firsthand. And the diffusion of general knowledge about museums and what they do could grow, to their benefit.

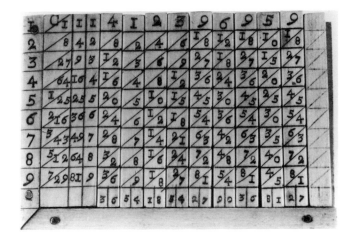

Where Museums Are Today

The legacy of the past and the shape of the future put museums today at the beginning of an era of considerable opportunity and challenge. There is a burgeoning museum movement in America, inspired by the values that museums espouse. People are making the commitment of museums their own personal commitment, and at the same time they are viewing museums with increased affection and appreciation. Museums have always been places for people, but despite long-standing public interest, there is nothing in the past to compare to the current lively enthusiasm Americans have for their museums. The sense of community among museums and their common identity as pluralistic institutions continue to evolve. As the open, democratic nature of museums becomes more emphatic, the relationship of museums to the rest of society—institutions and individuals alike—becomes even stronger.

It is the contention of this commission that museums have a twofold task today. We have described the forces of change in society that are most likely to affect museums, and it is imperative that the museum community recognize and participate in them. We have also described the contributions museums can make to the quality of the human experience, and we believe there must be a purposeful movement toward the full realization of that potential.

These two activities must exist in balance for museums to thrive; they are the inseparable prerequisites for a meaningful future. Attention to societal change is important because those who support, lead and work in museums cannot afford to be oblivious to the connection their institutions have to the rest of American life. They must be

Demographic Trends and Museums

The Sun Belt is where it's happening. More than 90 percent of the nation's population growth since 1980 has occurred in the southern and western states. Between the 1980 census and 1984, Florida, Texas and California each gained more than 500,000 people; those same states accounted for more than half the nation's total growth between 1960 and 1980. The population of western states together increased by 54 percent in the last two decades. In Texas alone the population shot up from 9.5 million people in 1960 to 14.2 million in 1980.

As the U.S. population shifts south and west, museums in those areas are growing rapidly. Since 1964, 30 new art museums have been built or are in the advanced stages of planning in the western states. Six more museums have at least doubled in size, and seven have been expanded or refurbished. The number of all types of museums in Texas has increased sixfold in the last 15 years—from 106 to more than 650. Florida is also experiencing a flowering in museums that matches its population growth. The Florida Division of Cultural Affairs estimates that there are 30 new museums in the state since 1964—an increase of 67 percent in 20 years.

It is clear that as people build new communities, they build new museums. The *Museum Universe Survey* published in 1979 counted nearly 5,000 museums in the United States, and there are strong indications that that number will continue to grow. A survey conducted by Louis Harris for the National Research Center for the Arts concludes that 87 percent of all adult Americans believe that arts and cultural events are an essential part of community life. The same survey reports that cultural institutions are shedding their long-held image of elitism; nearly three-quarters of the adults surveyed wanted more cultural programming at the local level. The growth of museums in areas of rapid population growth testifies to the significance of museums to community life and helps assure that the nation's collections are accessible to large numbers of citizens.

The Census Bureau projects continued growth in the Sun Belt. Between 1980 and 2000 the western states, Texas and Florida are expected to show population increases of 45, 46 and 79 percent respectively. Their residents can look forward to more and better museums.

able to distinguish those changes that most directly affect museums, for both the long and short terms. More to the point, museums must participate in the continuum, not simply observe it or react to it. The structure of museums and the way they build their relationships with their communities and other institutions must be in harmony with the times.

There must be harmony, too, between this awareness of external conditions and the strong sense of internal identity that museums, as a community, have only begun to clarify. Although we speak with pride and satisfaction of the sense of unity among museums, we must remember that it is still new and still growing. There are considerable opportunities for museums to use that unity to advocate the essential nature of the service they perform.

To help museums begin the task, this commission has looked carefully at American museums as they exist today, as they have evolved in the recent past, as we think they might develop in the future. Each of us has a strong personal commitment to museums. We take considerable pride in their integrity, their intellectual independence and the unique nature of their value to American life. We could easily spend the rest of our report extolling the virtues of institutions for which we, like the public, have great affection, but that would be both inappropriate and unproductive. Our challenge, after all, is to attempt leadership and vision for the future. Museums encourage careful thought, and a strong point of the museum community has always been its capacity for self-evaluation.

We have therefore singled out seven conditions in museums today that need to be approached with fresh insight.

First, *there are pressing needs with regard to the growth, organization and care of museum collections.* Museum staff, trustees and supporters must turn closer attention to the current and future condition of the objects that are the heart of our museums.

Museums have not realized their full potential as educational institutions. Despite a long-standing and serious commitment to their function as institutions of informal learning, there is a troublesome gap between reality and potential that must be addressed by policy makers in education and museums.

The times demand strong, forward-thinking leadership for museums. *Their organizational structure, in particular their system of governance, needs reexamination to ensure that it will meet the demands of the future.*

The museum community has never adequately described or aggressively promoted the significant contributions museums make to the quality of the human experience. In their own best interests, and in the interests of the public they serve, museums need to market their assets more thoroughly and effectively.

The diversity of the community of museums is not fully representative of the diversity of the society it seeks to serve. In their governance and staffing, museums have much to gain by making a commitment to greater diversity.

There is no adequate profile of American museums. As a mature and public profession, the museum field has an obligation to set up a mechanism for continuously collecting and analyzing data about museums.

Finally, *the economic situation in museums is extremely fragile.* Future economic stability is an issue that both museums and their supporters must address, for financial health is essential if museums are to fulfill their responsibilities and satisfy the expectations society holds for them.

We hope our recommendations will point to opportunities on the horizon and guide both individual museums and the museum community toward long-term solutions. They are directed to museum leaders and other museum professionals, in museums of all types and sizes, to leaders in business and foundations, museum trustees, educators, government officials at all levels, the media and leaders of a vast array of community service organizations that share the "independent sector" with museums.

There are two types of recommendations. In chapters 2 and 3 we establish two priorities for action—the growth, organization and care of museum collections and the function of museums as institutions of learning. In chapters 4 through 7 we propose avenues for taking action that involve stimulating effective leadership and an atmosphere of professionalism, extending collaborative efforts with other institutions at a variety of levels, increasing public awareness of the essential service museums provide and working toward long-term financial stability.

Our recommendations are not intended to be read in isolation. Their meaning derives wholly from the context in which they are presented; the ideas we express in the following chapters are as important as the recommendations that grew out of them.

◆ RECOMMENDATION 1: In planning for the growth of its collection, we urge each museum to set clear, rational and appropriate goals for the contribution it can make to the stewardship of our cultural and natural heritage. It is important that every museum collect both carefully and purposefully. Each must exercise care by collecting within its capacity to house and preserve the objects, artifacts and specimens in its stewardship; each must collect purposefully by continuing its own traditions of quality and diversity. A periodic review of the collections policy will ensure that it is in keeping with current professional standards and the purposes of the institution.

◆ RECOMMENDATION 2: The aggregate national significance of museum collections, the vast numbers of objects that might potentially be collected and the limited resources available to museums mandate that careful thought be given to their growth and care. We urge museums with similar interests to develop the elements of coordinated policies on what objects, artifacts and specimens are to be collected, how and by which institutions. Such policies, when appropriate, should be self-governing policies developed by the professional organizations within each discipline.

◆ RECOMMENDATION 3: In the belief that America's museum collections are a national resource which merits a strong federal commitment, we urge the acceleration of the federal initiative in collections care and organization. We applaud the recent interest of policy makers at the federal level in these critical activities, but we urge them to consider these steps as just the beginning of an effort to meet the actual needs of all museums. The Institute of Museum Services, the National Endowments for the Arts and the Humanities, the National Science Foundation and the National Museum Act all must share in the commitment.

◆ RECOMMENDATION 4: The lack of information about the number, location and condition of objects, artifacts and specimens in the nation's museums is a handicap to adequate care and maintenance of these collections and to scholarly progress in general. We urge a planning study to determine the feasibility of a national series of

inventories of museum collections, organized and conducted by discipline.

These inventories will be the basis for sound future collections management as well as for the development of sound collections policies. The various museum service organizations should collaborate in the planning study.

In addition to proposing a mechanism for carrying out inventories, the study should initiate the development of an information-sharing system for all museums that could eventually include data about acquisition and disposal of objects; research activity; use of collections by educational institutions, print and broadcast media; and sharing museum collections through loans and exhibitions.

◆ RECOMMENDATION 5: Education is a primary purpose of American museums. To assure that the educational function is integrated into all museum activities, museums need to look carefully at their internal operational structures. Collaborative approaches to public programs that include educational as well as scholarly and exhibition components facilitate achieving the full educational mission of museums.

◆ RECOMMENDATION 6: We urge a high priority for research into the ways people learn in museums. Continuing, systematic research into these unique processes and mechanisms is the key to the success of the museum as an environment for learning. Research is also needed to guide the introduction of computers and other electronic technology into museum learning. Universities linked with consortiums of museums in particular fields might provide a mechanism for implementing these studies.

◆ RECOMMENDATION 7: We recommend that the AAM and other professional education and museum organizations convene a national colloquium to begin an effective dialogue about the mutually enriching relationship museums and schools should have. We urge that the new consideration of the museum-school partnership involve leaders at all levels, with participation from government, business, the academic community, education and museums. This colloquium should consider the value of collaboration between museums and schools, the issues that need fresh approaches for the future and the practical means by which mutual goals can be realized at the state and local levels.

◆ RECOMMENDATION 8: We urge that museums continue to build on their success as centers of learning by providing high-quality educational experiences for people of all ages, but, in recognition of the increasing median age of our population, that they pay new attention to their programs for adults. Museum professionals must consider ways to introduce their institutions to the adult public as sources of intellectual enrichment, as places where learning can be spontaneous and personal and as opportunities for growth and thinking as well as seeing.

◆ RECOMMENDATION 9: Effective leadership for museums emerges from the ability of trustees to shape and guide the missions of their institutions. In the interest of making governance work better, we ask that a special, independent task force of trustees, directors and leaders of other nonprofit institutions with similar governance structures be convened at the initiative of the American Association of Museums. It should assess the quality of governance of American museums, examining such matters as the board-staff relationship and the selection and composition of boards. It should also identify the kinds of assistance that would equip both trustees and staff to provide the leadership museums will need in the future.

◆ RECOMMENDATION 10: Museum work merits professional compensation. If the salaries for professional staff in museums do not increase, the museum profession and museums nationwide will suffer the loss of talented people qualified to perform demanding and complex functions. We urge that each museum develop responsible compensation policies and practices that bring its salaries and benefits into line with professional work for which similar education and experience are required.

To describe the museum work force more completely, the museum community needs a professional personnel study that presents salary information and describes working conditions in the context of geographic location, training, experience, and level and nature of responsibility. This information is essential to a better understanding of the caliber of professional needed to run this country's museums. This study should be initiated by the American Association of Museums working in cooperation with other museum service organizations.

◆ RECOMMENDATION 11: We strongly believe the museum community must address the underrepresentation of minorities in the museum work force generally and the underrepresentation of women in the higher levels of management. It is the obligation of inherently pluralistic institutions such as museums to ensure that their organizational structures reflect cultural diversity and equal opportunity. The museum community should explore ways to interest minority young people in museum work at the high school level through special programs designed to direct them toward undergraduate and graduate academic disciplines that lead to museum careers. Boards of trustees and directors should give high priority to hiring qualified minorities and women in positions of leadership and authority and providing opportunities for them to advance up the career ladder.

Professional museum organizations can help both minorities and women by asserting that greater opportunity for these groups is a sign of high professional standards and by serving as networks of information and support.

◆ RECOMMENDATION 12: In the firm belief that size is not a criterion for excellence, we encourage programs that provide information and training for professionals and volunteers in small and developing museums. The education of staff enables museums to fulfill their obligations to their collections and their public. We suggest the following areas of emphasis: the care and maintenance of collections; governance, policy and planning; fund raising and membership development; and public programming.

◆ RECOMMENDATION 13: Through the appropriate professional organizations or a collaboration among them, the museum community must set up a permanent mechanism for collecting, analyzing and disseminating data about museums—their numbers and locations, their facilities and finances, their personnel and trustees, their activities and attendance. Policy makers both inside and outside the museum field must have current and comprehensive data on the museum field to guide their decisions. The availability of this information will aid all who strive to meet the needs of museums and communicate both the needs and the services of these important institutions to others.

◆ RECOMMENDATION 14: In a world of diminishing resources, collaboration among museums and between museums and other organizations will be increasingly obligatory. Rather than opting for joint programs through necessity, museums must take the lead in such efforts, for they offer many benefits in addition to economic efficiency. Collaboration can enhance the effectiveness and community visibility of museums. In their endeavor to meet the future positively, we urge that museums actively seek ways of working together and with other community organizations.

◆ RECOMMENDATION 15: A national program should be established to strengthen the public's awareness of the value of museums and to cultivate public commitment to museums as institutions that provide essential services to society. The American Association of Museums, in cooperation with other national museum organizations, should initiate this public awareness campaign to celebrate the collective vitality of our nation's museums and encourage the public to use and support museums as community resources and sources of personal enjoyment and enlightenment.

◆ RECOMMENDATION 16: Museums should increase their efforts toward achieving a more secure financial base for the future through a combination of sound management, self-help and appeals for public and private support. The benefits museums bring to a community and the nation must be demonstrated, and government officials must be more aware of their responsibility in the partnership of financial support. In particular, the necessity for federal leadership in commitment to museums as irreplaceable national resources must be aggressively and persistently emphasized. To generate a more balanced support for all facets of museum programs and operations, the museum community must explain its needs to government officials at all levels and to leaders in corporations and foundations. At the same time, museums should vigorously pursue cost-saving opportunities and creative ventures to increase earned income. They must continue to strive for the best in management practices.

2　Stewards of a Common Wealth

Even the sleekest, most up-to-date kitchens are sometimes adorned with objects of the past. Above the microwave oven is a display of utensils from the 1930s, purchased in an antique shop because they were reminiscent of the owner's childhood. Pink and green Depression glassware, once sold at the dime store but now available only through a community of collectors, lines an open shelf above the food processor and the electric coffee maker. And biscuit tins from the 1890s—ordinary tins once filled with ordinary biscuits—are given the care and respect one would expect for objects that command a substantial price.

Collecting is a fundamental human trait. Our homes contain things of the past because they are a source of nostalgia, of connection to a life we knew or our parents told us about. We collect stamps, postcards, coins, family photographs and heirlooms, and we do it for intensely personal reasons—to surround ourselves with objects we like, to make a connection to other places and other times, to satisfy the urge for material possession.

For museums the act of collecting is more than an institutional expression of a human trait. It is our society's cumulative effort to save ourselves, our history, our natural surroundings, our technological and creative endeavors. Although every museum collects for the same fundamental reason, the collecting patterns of each one are fueled by different incentives—a connoisseur's fascination, a curator's scholarship, a scientist's thirst for knowledge. Sometimes civic pride inspires a historical society to save the material evidence of a community's past. Machines that were turning points in scientific thought or technological development still work their wonders in science-

technology centers. Zoos and botanical gardens often hold the only survivors of plants or animals that have disappeared from the wild. And the special tastes and interests of private collectors have given this country's art museums a wealth of objects representing the whole of civilization's artistic heritage. The rich collections in American museums have diverse origins, and that gives our museums their democratic character.

Most museum collections have been shaped by special interests or particular needs. For this reason, museums are fiercely independent entities. But there is an aggregate as well as an individual significance, and that aggregate—our nation's common wealth—has been an important perspective of this commission. Museum collections, in the aggregate, represent the whole diversity of the world's cultural, scientific and natural heritage. We believe the museum community has not adequately emphasized that aggregate significance or the cumulative effort that museum collections represent.

Why take this broader view? Because recognizing the aggregate significance of museum collections focuses the distinctive, essential service museums perform for society and makes their needs visible and critical to the public. It was clear during our open forums and colloquiums that even people who are not closely connected with museums know that collections are the essence of the contribution museums make to society. Our discussions often revolved around the central nature of collections and the special power of the object. The objects museums hold in trust for the public are, after all, what distinguishes them from other cultural institutions. This unequivocal emphasis makes it all the more urgent that the museum community attend to issues involving the collections in their stewardship. We identify in particular the need for a rational approach to the growth of collections and the need for attention to their care, organization and research.

Collections Growth: Issues of Size, Shape and Scope

It makes sense to begin our discussion with the growth of collections, because the scale of future care and maintenance issues will be determined at least in part by the number of objects in the nation's museums. "More than a billion" is the usual educated guess. In its recently completed inventory, the Smithsonian Institution alone recorded 100 million objects and predicted an annual growth rate of 3 percent. The Association of Systematics Collections estimates that there are close to 600 million biological specimens in museum and university collections, a number that is also increasing by 3 percent each year.

In most museums, however, only a small proportion of the collection is on exhibit at any one time. In natural history museums, collections are often maintained primarily for research use; the San Diego Museum of Man, for example, exhibits just 3 percent of its total holdings. In other museums, the number of objects in the collection is so large that choices must be made; the Munson-Williams-Proctor Institute in Utica, New York, for example, exhibits only one percent of its permanent collection.

Every museum may not experience rapid growth, but it is virtually impossible to find one in which the size of collections is static. Four vastly different museums offer illustration. At the McKinley Museum of History, Science and Industry in Canton, Ohio, the number of objects went from 55,000 in 1978 to 60,000 in 1983, a 9 percent increase. The Albright-Knox Art Gallery in Buffalo, New York, saw its collections increase by 14 percent in that period, from 10,500 objects to 12,000. Small, newer museums grow even faster. The collections of the Southeast Arkansas Arts and Science Center in Pine Bluff, a museum founded in 1968, grew from 200 objects to 600 in five years, for a growth rate of 200 percent. Perhaps the most dramatic rates of growth occur in science and natural history museums. The Florida State Museum in Gainesville added more than one million objects and specimens to its collection between 1978 and 1983, a 31 percent increase in total holdings.

The cumulative collecting enterprise is fundamental to museums, and it must continue. Moreover, American museums are still young. Though a few institutions were established in the years before the Civil War, the great surge in museum founding came in the late 19th century. The aggregate museum collection has been growing for just more than 100 years, and it must continue to increase if museums are to fulfill their missions well. Institutions with living collections have a special mandate; they must propagate plants and animals if the species are to survive. Natural history museums must collect actively to preserve examples of rapidly disappearing plants and animals. As our time on earth lengthens, history museums will inevitably increase their holdings. As technological change accelerates, science-technology centers must keep pace. And art museums must ensure that their collections are balanced chronicles of human creativity.

For individual museums, a certain amount of growth is necessary to ensure quality; a static collection is not likely to be excellent in esthetic, scientific or intellectual terms. A museum cannot contribute to a body of knowledge or responsibly enlighten the public if its trustees and staff do not devote adequate attention to shaping the collection and improving it.

But growth presents some troublesome issues for museums. Most obvious is the simple matter of care: the larger the collection, the greater the strains on the museum's resources. Recommendations on the size of individual museum collections are best addressed at close range by each institution; so, too, are most matters of scope.

In fact, the adoption of clear collections policies in individual museums is a prerequisite to rational growth. A positive trend in recent decades is the care with which museum staff and trustees have defined the limits of their collecting interests by adopting formal statements about goals and procedures for acquiring and deaccessioning objects. Many small museums, however, have not yet taken this step. Among the museums in our monitoring system, not a single one with a budget of less than $100,000 reported having a formal policy.

Museum Ethics, a statement on ethical standards and practices published in 1978 by the American Association of Museums, clearly describes the necessity for collections policies, and the paramount importance of the issue has led the AAM's Accreditation Commission to require that each museum have such a policy in order to be accredited. With a clear policy statement, decisions about collecting are less likely to be arbitrary, more likely to be made with a practical consideration of the museum's mission.

But it is not enough simply to have a policy. It is our sense, borne out by the experiences of the accreditation process, that many collections policies are too vague and too general. They are not serious attempts to evaluate the museum's existing collections and its present and potential resources. A more critical problem is the failure of many museums to review and revise their policies. A regular reassessment of collections policies and the deaccessioning of objects that no longer relate to the goals of the museum are absolutely essential if a museum is to contribute with integrity to scholarship and public understanding.

Decisions about collecting are the most crucial choices museum staff and trustees make, and while they must be made by each institution individually, they should no longer be made in isolation or competition. The issues in collecting and growth facing museums of all kinds today demand, at the least, cooperative consideration.

Some history museums, for example, are beginning to recognize their responsibility for collecting contemporary objects so that the everyday life of ordinary people in the late 20th century can be fairly represented in the museums of tomorrow. Yet nothing is less likely to be preserved than the disposable items that seem so prolific to those who use them and throw them away. Where will tomorrow's curators find, for example, the Adidas jogging shoes, granola bars and Darth Vader T-shirts that mark the popular culture of the 1980s—unless museums collect them? But do all museums need to collect them?

Local and regional history museums and historical societies are now debating the issue of collecting the contemporary in their communities. Recently a mid-20th-century diner was added to the collection of the Henry Ford Museum and Greenfield Village in Dearborn, Michigan. The concern is also illustrated by the Smithsonian's acquisition of such television artifacts as the set from "M*A*S*H" and Archie Bunker's chair from "All in the Family." While ours is not the first generation to consider collecting the present for the future, it is the first to face the issue in the

Collecting for the Future

We all know that even the humblest of our material possessions may someday be prized as samples of life in the late 20th century. But how do you go about collecting contemporary objects, and documenting them in some rational way, to make sure they'll be available for future generations? In the late 1970s a series of four conferences in Sweden addressed this question. The resulting report, published in English as *Today for Tomorrow: Museum Documentation of Contemporary Society in Sweden by Acquisition of Objects*, warned that "if documentation [of today's society] is neglected, we run the risk of depriving [future] generations of their history." In implementing the report's recommendations, Sweden became the only country in the world to undertake the formidable task of systematically collecting and documenting the present for the future.

Known as SAMDOK (an acronym for the Swedish word *samtidsdokumentation*, meaning "contemporary documentation"), this national system of collection and documentation is administered by a secretariat housed at the Nordiska Museum in Stockholm. The program is carried out according to "sector" and "milieu." A sector is defined as an aggregate of related physical, social and/or economic structures such as the glass industry, winter sports, the ecological movement or women's fashions. Because the number of possible sectors could be infinite, SAMDOK recommends a checklist to guide decisions about collecting. Three types of milieu are documented: the home milieu, the working milieu and the public and commercial milieu.

To increase efficiency and reduce duplication, SAMDOK distributes responsibility for collecting. The national museums collect within their area of specialization. Regional and municipal museums collect samples of contemporary life typical of their geographic area but not documented anywhere else in the country.

Five of Sweden's large cultural history museums have established Homes Pool, a cooperative system for documenting homelife developed by the Nordiska Museum's Department of Field Research. Each year the museums rotate the responsibility for documenting a "normal household" within their respective districts. Households are chosen in consultation with the SAMDOK secretariat and the Homes Pool. Museum staff members photograph every room and storage cabinet; they make drawings of furniture arrangements and list all household items. They also collect information about buildings, fixtures, technical equipment, furniture and the household members themselves— occupation, education, eating habits and recreation. The museum also acquires the objects the household has bought during the year, either from the household itself or on the open market. Each museum accepts responsibility for conserving the objects it acquires and makes them available to other museums for research or exhibition. The SAMDOK secretariat maintains a data bank on all the findings of the investigating museum for use by other museums in the Homes Pool.

Collecting the present is necessary if museums of the 21st century are to understand and represent our own times. With SAMDOK, the Swedes have developed a comprehensive and sophisticated approach to this mammoth task.

The Species Survival Plan

In most of the world's wild places, animal populations are declining. The American Association of Zoological Parks and Aquariums (AAZPA) explains that trends far too advanced to be reversed will cause the expected loss of many creatures in the next century. At least 20 percent of some 4 million species of animals are in danger of extinction. Some of them — the whooping crane, the black-footed ferret, the tiger and the Asiatic elephant—will exist only in zoos, aquariums or nature preserves.

Today these institutions are preparing for the next century by directing their efforts to propagating their own animals. The AAZPA has developed and distributed a formal Species Survival Plan (SSP) to strengthen and coordinate captive programs so that zoos and aquariums can assist in the worldwide effort to preserve vanishing species.

Propagation of species is difficult in most zoos, however, because of crowded quarters. North American zoos average less than 55 acres, only part of which is devoted to actual animal space; together, they constitute less than 20,000 acres. Thus sudden epidemic disease or natural catastrophe may wipe out the efforts of any one zoo committed to breeding a rare animal. One solution is cooperation, and breeding loans among zoos are now commonplace. Chinese alligators, gorillas, Indian rhinos, Bali mynas and other rare animals are transferred from zoo to zoo not for purposes of exhibition or even an individual zoo's benefit but to enhance the chances of propagation for the welfare of the species concerned.

One important element of the plan is a computer-based information system for animals in captivity called the International Species Inventory System (ISIS). More than 51,000 living mammals and birds have been inventoried — and indirectly, tens of thousands of their ancestors—in more than 150 institutions in North America, plus a growing number in Europe, Australia and South America. ISIS collects information on age, sex, parentage, place of birth and circumstances of death. The computer program is now being redesigned to accommodate increasingly sophisticated information. Basic laboratory data on normal individual animals, like blood chemistry for example, will soon help in disease detection. The system already has data on 10,000 animal blood samples.

The AAZPA and the entire living collections community have developed and continue to support model cooperative approaches to collections inventory and ultimately the preservation of wildlife. Once the inventory has been completed, the AAZPA will be in a position to direct the future survival of captive populations—a monumental task but one very near realization. ISIS will continue to expand on two major fronts. The inclusion of reptiles and amphibians in the inventory has long been planned and is now under way. And the number of participating institutions is growing. Foresight and hard work on the part of living collections professionals will continue to save a few of the endangered species of animals throughout the world from extinction, and similar efforts are beginning for selected plant species.

context of a society with such an abundance of material culture.

Other kinds of museums face equally challenging dilemmas related to growth. The diminishing numbers of available works of art from previous centuries may force some art museums to redefine the scope of their collections; rising prices may also compel new priorities. In science-technology centers, one challenge is to document and anticipate technological change. Just as a National Air and Space Museum could not have been imagined 30 years ago, there will surely be museums in the next century that collect artifacts we do not know about today.

Zoos are leading the way in developing shared collections responsibilities. The nature of their new mandate to breed and preserve species has made collaboration an absolute necessity. Similarly, institutions with biological collections tend to divide the collecting turf, both formally and informally, so as to preserve as comprehensive a sample of the natural world as possible. History museums sometimes define their collecting policies in light of the activities of other institutions, such as research libraries and historical societies, which also hold historical evidence in the form of photographs, books, manuscripts and other archival material. But in most museum disciplines there is no coordinated, widely understood agreement or policy, on either the national or international level, about what should be collected and by whom.

We believe that the notion of the aggregate significance of museum collections should be a guiding principle here. The diversity of museums with individual interests is an advantage, for together they can join in a single, larger purpose. Within the prescribed mission of museums—preserving and interpreting our heritage—there is room for a great deal of variation in scale and specialization. Among some kinds of museums, sharing information may be more feasible and practical than in others, but in general, if information about collecting activity were shared more systematically, at the very least within disciplines, the burden on individual institutions might be alleviated and their individual missions and public significance would be strengthened. It is our conviction that the museum community must begin to look at its collections as having an aggregate importance, the ultimate goal being not individual possession, but understanding, knowledge and appreciation.

With this view in mind, the museum community must move toward the development of coordinated policies on the national and international levels. Individual collections policies should be widely disseminated among museums in each discipline, so actions may be taken to assure that collecting generally will benefit not only individual interests but also the needs of the entire museum community and the public it serves. In reviewing collections policies, each museum must now consider the gaps in general scholarship and coordination with other institutions. Establishing complementary priorities will help museums in each field assemble the best possible aggregation of objects, artifacts and specimens.

♦ RECOMMENDATION 1: In planning for the growth of its collection, we urge each museum to set clear, rational and appropriate goals for the contribution it can make to the stewardship of our cultural and natural heritage. It is important that every museum collect both carefully and purposefully. Each must exercise care by collecting within its capacity to house and preserve the objects, artifacts and specimens in its stewardship; each must collect purposefully by continuing its own traditions of quality and diversity. A periodic review of the collections policy will ensure that it is in keeping with current professional standards and the purposes of the institution.

♦ RECOMMENDATION 2: The aggregate national significance of museum collections, the vast numbers of objects that might potentially be collected and the limited resources available to museums mandate that careful thought be given to their growth and care. We urge museums with similar interests to develop the elements of coordinated policies on what objects, artifacts and specimens are to be collected, how and by which institutions. Such policies, when appropriate, should be self-governing policies developed by the professional organizations within each discipline.

Collections Care: A Chronic, Unquantified Problem

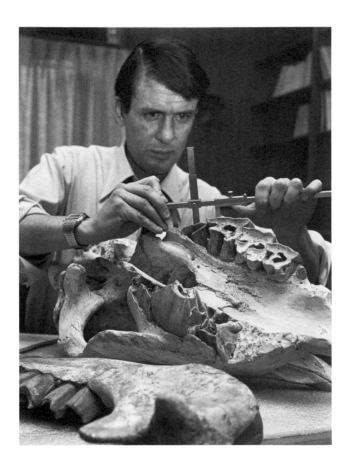

In a 1982 *Christian Science Monitor* article, David Hugh Smith vividly described a perennial museum concern: "There's a silent thief stealing away with millions of dollars of art work each year. The thief's name? Poor conservation." The same villain is at work in museums of history and natural history. Being collected and stored in a museum is no guarantee that any object will, in fact, be preserved in perpetuity. Some things quite naturally disintegrate over time—delicate watercolors, for example, or leather bookbindings. Others may be damaged and require stabilization or repair to prevent further deterioration. The scientific examination and treatment of museum objects and the study of the optimum environments for their preservation constitute the field of study known as conservation.

But conservation is just one aspect of the unquantified problem of collections care. Museums have both ethical and legal obligations to maintain and manage the objects entrusted to them, and that involves all the activities necessary to preserve objects in perpetuity, to gain intellectual control over them (by acquiring and recording information about them) and to make them accessible to scholars. Care connotes everything from providing controlled environmental conditions to ensuring adequate security, maintaining necessary catalog records and repairing damage.

It is no easy task. The environmental requirements of the millions of objects in the nation's biological collections alone are vastly complex. Some kinds of biological samples are stored in liquid nitrogen at very low temperatures, others in fluids. Some must be protected from insects, others are as resistant to change as the rocks in which they have been imbedded. An art museum might have contemporary metal sculpture, fragile 17th-century ceramics and 19th-century photographic prints, all to be housed in the same storage areas and exhibited in adjacent galleries despite vastly different requirements for care in relation to light, temperature and humidity. Differences are even greater among objects in anthropology and history museums, from Hopi Indian baskets to lace doilies to leather harnesses to dulcimers to jet aircraft.

There is little precise information about the condition of the objects in the aggregate American museum collection and the magnitude of the needs in regard to their care. But David Hugh Smith is correct in assuming that the scope is staggering. The 62 museums in the commission's monitoring system reported what we believe to be typical problems: inadequate storage space, substandard environmental conditions, poor security, insufficient staff, inaccessible or unaffordable conservation treatment services and, of course, limited funds.

Some museums have surveyed the needs of their collections; most have not. Many lack up-to-date inventories. Computerized record keeping—a topic we address in greater detail later in this chapter—is relatively new to most museums. Many small museums—and even some larger ones—have a more fundamental problem: the absence of thorough, consistent documentation about the objects in their care, for reasons ranging from limited staff training to budgetary restraints. Many said that their most urgent need was a seemingly simple one: to catalog information about objects in their collections. The sheer volume of information—data that are essential to knowledge and understanding of the objects—poses challenges for museums of all kinds and sizes.

The point is not to argue that care and organization should be a priority, because the museum community knows that. The point, we believe, is to move from agreement that collections care is a large-scale problem to finding a way to make the problem manageable and ultimately solvable.

The Scale of the Problem

Through the efforts of professional organizations such as the American Institute for Conservation (AIC) and the National Institute for the Conservation of Cultural Property (NIC), we do know something, but not enough, about specific needs related to the condition of objects in some kinds of museum collections. In the formal proposal for the establishment of the NIC, the severity of the problem was stated bluntly:

> Although interest in the arts has increased, the United States still is without a national policy or plan for conservation, the informed, skilled and ethical care of cultural patrimony. It is virtually the only major nation in the world without a coordinated effort in this regard.

State Inventories of Museum Collections

A statewide inventory of museum collections is still a dream in most parts of the country, but in Indiana it has been a reality for some time. The computerized inventory project of the Association of Indiana Museums is now undergoing a 10-year evaluation, and, according to Nikki Black, project director, the future of collections management in the Hoosier State is very bright indeed.

Since the statewide inventory was begun in 1973, data on more than 250,000 art, history and ethnology objects, from 106 Indiana museums, have been entered on a computer in a consistent format that makes it readily retrievable for use by museums, scholars and other researchers. The project has several purposes. Like most states, Indiana has a large number of county historical societies, each with some excellent artifacts—quilts, horse gear, woodworking tools — but none is large or important enough for its collection to be well known. The inventory assures that significant or appropriate pieces in out-of-the-way places will not be overlooked in exhibition planning. In addition, it has enabled the association to respond to numerous research requests. When the National Portrait Gallery recently asked states to provide information on all portraits in public collections for its *Catalog of American Portraits*, most states had difficulty complying, but Indiana was able to respond with ease and confidence.

Other states have inventoried portions of collections or particular types of collections. In Maine, for instance, an inventory project is part of a large effort designed to inform people about the state. As in Indiana, Maine has scores of historical societies and small museums with fine collections, but objects in the larger institutions are the only ones that have been known to researchers and used by exhibit planners. To rectify this imbalance, an inventory team crossed the state, visiting all museums, historical societies and historic sites and photographing and cataloging some 1,200 decorative and fine arts objects. The resulting slide collection is being used to teach Maine history, and seminars funded by the Maine Humanities Council are training schoolteachers to use objects in the classroom. Future plans include putting the inventory data on computer so that it will be as accessible to exhibit planners and researchers as the collections in Indiana's museums.

The need for a national plan has been discussed for more than 30 years. In the late l950s the Association of Art Museum Directors endorsed a written proposal for a national conservation institute. Yet the extent of the problems in collections care was still apparent a decade later when the Belmont Report observed that most museums were simply "presiding over the steady deterioration of that which they have been instituted to preserve." Still later, a l980 study of conservation treatment facilities by the National Conservation Advisory Council (now the NIC) reported a variety of options for obtaining conservation services but emphasized that the needs of the nation's museums were still not being met, the number of objects treated in a given year being only a minute percentage of those requiring immediate attention.

These studies and plans have dealt only with conservation—just one aspect of collections care. If one considers storage, climate control, inventory, cataloging and other needs, the problem is magnified. *Museums USA* (l974), the last report that addressed the care of collections in any detail, reported troublesome trends. In most of the museums surveyed, the expenditures were not considered adequate to meet immediate needs. For conservation alone, directors estimated that an average increase of 58 percent in operating expenditures would be required.

Early in 1984, at the request of Congress, the Institute of Museum Services contracted with the American Association of Museums to assess conservation needs in American museums. This study, conducted in cooperation with both AIC and NIC, will provide the quantitative data necessary to begin setting a responsible policy for adequate care of the nation's collections.

As with many of the tasks facing museums in the next few decades, we see both an internal and an external face to the problem of collections care. An internal dynamic determines the low priority often given collections care within an institution, while external perceptions limit the resources available to museums.

We are concerned that collections care and maintenance are not a high enough priority within the museum community, among museum trustees, directors and staff. In competition with more visible public programs and popular special exhibitions, which offer immediate, tangible rewards to the museum and for which funding is more often available, the less glamourous, be-

hind-the-scenes activities can too easily be pushed aside. In the pressure to serve the public's immediate enthusiasms, it is perhaps too easy to slight its ultimate best interests.

The public's enthusiasm for museums has been heightened lately by the increasing number of circulating special exhibitions, a phenomenon that shows no sign of abating. In many respects, these exhibitions have been good for museums. Since they use borrowed objects as well as material from the museum's own collections, they enable a museum to expand its subject matter, interests and appeal. They are difficult to resist because they can attract increased attendance, generate earned income and build a strong and committed membership base.

But there are valid concerns that special exhibitions can distract museums from the fundamental activities of collections care and sap the intellectual, as well as the physical, energy of directors and curators. Philippe de Montebello, director of the Metropolitan Museum of Art in New York, which has enjoyed its share of "blockbusters" and popular special exhibitions, has warned that

> basic museum work—conservation, research, cataloging, scholarly publications—gives way to the effort that goes into realizing special events. . . . The time and effort of a museum's curatorial, conservation and administrative staff are displaced from a concern for fundamentals to the support of the special event.

Special exhibitions have other hidden costs. They cause wear-and-tear on buildings that are already expensive to maintain. Although the potential for earned income is tempting, it may not always be realized. In short, the price of public popularity may be too high if special exhibitions keep museum staff from the essential day-to-day activities of caring for museum collections.

Special exhibitions aside, collections care is still not as high an internal priority as it should be. Eighty-four percent of the directors surveyed for *Museums USA* considered conservation and preservation a very important function of museums, yet only 8 percent gave it as a top budgetary priority for the future. We asked the museums in our monitoring system about the proportion of their budgets assigned to conservation—again, just one aspect of collections care—and learned that it is minuscule, from zero to 4.5 percent. The director of a history museum told us, "I would like to see more staff awareness that our collection consists of one-of-a-kind items that must be treated with great care. They have to realize that once these things have deteriorated to the point that they cannot be restored, we have lost an important part of our heritage."

The mixed signals conveyed by museums themselves must be at least partly responsible for the lack of interest among private and public funding sources in supporting such basic activities as storage, the treatment of objects and climate control. With some notable exceptions, support from foundations and corporations for these basic operating activities is meager in contrast to that available for popular, highly visible programs and exhibitions. The federal government has made some commitment to collections care, but the amount of support in no way meets the need. Policy makers either fail to understand the magnitude of collection needs or despair of ever being able to help solve such a monumental—and poorly quantified—problem.

Still, the current picture is not entirely gloomy. After the Belmont Report of 1969 recommended a substantially increased financial commitment to collections care, welcome changes in patterns of federal support have occurred. Since 1971 the Museum Program of the National Endowment for the Arts (NEA) has made more than $11 million in grants—primarily to art museums—for conservation planning, treatment, purchase of equipment, training of personnel, climate control, security and storage. Nearly half that amount has gone to training programs in art conservation, and about 30 percent of the funds have been designated for the conservation of specific objects. The NEA was also instrumental in supporting the founding and development of cooperative conservation centers around the country.

Valuable if limited federal support has also come from the National Museum Act (NMA), a small program administered by the Smithsonian Institution that has made grants to individuals for research in conservation. The amount of money available has always been small ($508,000 in grants for conservation to 51 recipients in fiscal year 1983), but the agency has had a steady commitment to research in conservation and to the continuing education of working professionals.

The National Science Foundation (NSF) has also supported the care and maintenance of a wide variety of scientific collections, its grants totaling about $4 million each year. In the four

years from 1978 to 1982, NSF funding for systematics and anthropological collections in museums and universities alone amounted to $10 million. Grants have supported conservation, storage and reorganization of collections, cataloging and inventory projects.

Two other federal agencies are just beginning to support basic collections-related activities. The Institute of Museum Services (IMS) began a pilot program of grants for conservation in fiscal year 1984. Through a grant to the AAM, the National Endowment for the Humanities (NEH) is studying the need for assistance among museums and historical organizations and will support collections care and maintenance in fiscal year 1985.

In all, however, the total annual commitment to collections care and maintenance by the five federal agencies that provide major support to museums is just over $7 million—a small amount when one considers that the estimated total operating budgets of America's museums in 1979 was nearly a billion dollars. Funding is particularly scarce for history museums and museums with living collections.

In the private sector, only a few foundations regularly support projects involving conservation, storage or documentation. The Foundation Center lists 36 private foundations as contributors to the care of collections; 21 grants were made to all types of museums in 1982.

Several major foundations—Mellon, Kress, Kresge—make the largest proportion of the grants. The A. W. Mellon Foundation awarded $22 million for conservation in 1975–82, nearly half the total awarded for that purpose by all foundations. An endowment from the Samuel H. Kress Foundation has supported the graduate program in conservation and the technology of works of art at the Institute of Fine Arts, New York University, while Kresge made grants to the National Gallery of Art for construction of a conservation analytical laboratory and renovation of other conservation facilities. Community and regional foundations are just beginning to make grants for collections care, but almost exclusively for art museums.

Funds from corporations are less readily available. In an informal poll of 10 large museums, we learned that none receives substantial corporate support for the care of collections. There was a general sense that corporations are not receptive to the idea of supporting relatively invisible activities in a museum. The director of a natural history museum told us, "We never really waged a campaign for the care of collections specifically—we consider this a part of the overall campaign to get money for the museum." The development officer of a history museum said, "We do receive some money from a large private foundation; we have tried to get money for conservation from corporations, but with no luck."

There are, of course, notable exceptions. Some businesses have included money for conservation work in grants for major exhibitions; Philip Morris' support of *The Vatican Collections: The Papacy and Art* is one example, and the restoration of paintings in the *El Greco of Toledo* exhibition funded by American Express is another. In a gallery at the Williams College Art Museum, conservators are restoring a Thomas Hart Benton mural, a project supported by the Equitable Life Assurance Society of the United States.

Most people know very little about the complexity of caring for the objects they so enjoy. To explain those needs should not be difficult for institutions that pride themselves on communicating with the public. The Williams College project is just one example of a successful effort to introduce the public to collections care. At the Museums at Stony Brook in 1982, an exhibition called *Dirty Linens* showed the intricacies of the care and handling of historic costumes and textiles. A taxidermist works on the spot in the Savage Hall of Zoology at the Buffalo Museum of Science; through windows into the laboratory, visitors can see specimens being prepared for display. And in perhaps the best publicized conservation effort, the work of art historian Pinin Brambilla Barcilon on the restoration of Leonardo's *Last Supper* has received wide press coverage in magazines as diverse as *Parade* and *National Geographic*.

◆ RECOMMENDATION 3: In the belief that America's museum collections are a national resource which merits a strong federal commitment, we urge the acceleration of the federal initiative in collections care and organization. We applaud the recent interest of policy makers at the federal level in these critical activities, but we urge them to consider these steps as just the beginning of an effort to meet the actual needs of all museums. The Institute of Museum Services, the National Endowments for the Arts and the Humanities, the National Science Foundation and the National Museum Act all must share in the commitment.

Catching Up with the Technological Age

The organization and documentation needs of collections—an integral part of collections care—are particularly critical problems. Acquiring and keeping information about objects are primary activities of museums. Without proper documentation, a museum has a limited story to tell. The development of rational policies about growth depends on the information museums have about existing collections. And adequate documentation is the key to quantifying the care and maintenance needs of collections. Moreover, museums are legally and ethically obligated to assemble certain basic information about their collections and to maintain it according to accepted professional standards. To make the job manageable, the rapid development of information processing and communications technologies offers many new opportunities that must not be ignored.

A computer's value in the documentation process arises from its ability to speed the creation, organization and retrieval of records. In addition to the collections management applications—catalog, inventory, loan, exhibition and insurance records—computers enable museums to use scarce resources effectively, plan exhibitions, carry out scholarly activities and avoid duplication in collecting. Computers serve other museum needs, too. In fact, museums are most likely to use computers for administrative operations such as accounting and financial records and membership and donor information.

There is no denying that the kind of computer assistance most museums need is costly; both the initial expense of hardware and software and the cost of maintaining a computer system once it is in place have been barriers to the use of computers by museums. There are major staffing requirements, too, that place further demands on overextended resources. In some respects, though, the prospects for museums and computers have never been better. As information management technology becomes more advanced, more accessible, more affordable and more applicable to museum work, museums with budgets of all sizes can consider some measure of computerization.

Some museums, especially large natural history museums, have been computerizing collections data for more than 20 years. In the 1960s several museums developed their own software systems, as there were no commercial packages that would mcct their special demands. The Smithsonian's SELGEM, and GRIPHOS, developed by a group of New York museums, were software packages designed to accommodate a large quantity of information about the variety of objects found in museums. Many museums have been using these systems long enough and with enough success that they have now adapted them to their special institutional needs.

Museums are working together to solve problems and to develop appropriate computer systems. The Museum Computer Network, Inc. (MCN), for instance, was the first association dedicated to helping museums take advantage of today's information technology. MCN attaches special importance to small museums, which have disproportionately large collections and serious information management needs. In Chicago the Museum of Science and Industry has just established the Information Technology Resource Center, a clearinghouse and support center that will help nonprofit organizations with information systems and telecommunications technologies.

Computer use is still not widespread, however. A 1982 survey conducted by the Art Museum Association of America (AMAA) found that 68 percent of the 362 responding art museums were not using computers. Twenty-five percent used computers housed elsewhere; 7 percent had in-house facilities. Only 16 percent were using computers for collections management. In 1983 the Print Council conducted a similar survey on the status of computerization of collection information in art museums and reported that 57 percent of museums did not have programming capability. Nearly half reported that some phase of computerization was under way. As in the AMAA study, most museums reported plans to add computers in the future.

Plans for computerizing museum collections range from preliminary discussions to definite decisions and implementation schedules. The University Art Museum at the University of Minnesota in Minneapolis, for example, is discussing with Control Data Corporation a plan to computerize information on the 10,000 objects in the museum's collection. On a larger scale, the Art Museum Association of America has begun ARTIS, a project to help museums use computer technology to meet administrative and collections needs.

Some museums are well beyond the implementation stage and are in the process of seeking to

Museum Computer Projects

More museums than ever are using computers in their operations. Computers help make financial, membership and development record keeping more efficient. They also provide a new dimension to educational programming. Very important for museums are the new possibilities computers offer for collections management. Of the scores of projects now in planning and pilot stages, these three are the most ambitious and have implications for the entire museum community.

■ *ARTIS.* The Art Museum Information System (ARTIS) is a software system designed and administered by the Art Museum Association of America. It has three components: a financial information system, a membership and development information system and a collections information system, which records data about objects, including description, artist, condition, location and subject fields. Information is also available about the collection as a whole, including accessions and deaccessions, loans, inventory control and conservation needs. Four museums—the Albright-Knox Art Gallery in Buffalo, New York; the Amon Carter Museum in Fort Worth, Texas; the Honolulu Academy of Arts in Honolulu, Hawaii; and the Toledo Museum of Art in Toledo, Ohio—are testing software that will be refined and available for purchase by museums in 1985.

■ *Art History Information Program.* In 1982 the J. Paul Getty Trust launched a study to determine how it could help improve access to information in art history through new technology. No institution had been able to address the complex problems of system compatibility involved in international coordination and information exchange. The trust has now made a major commitment in this area through its Art History Information Program The computerized, integrated information system being developed will link data bases of conservation, bibliographic, biographic, catalog and provenance information from art museums through the world.

■ *Collections Information System (CIS).* This integrated set of general applications is being designed to support the collections management needs of the Smithsonian Institution's 10 museums and zoo. These applications include documentation (cataloging and describing objects), live specimen management (an adjunct to documentation designed to meet the needs of living collections in zoos and botanical gardens), collections management (recording the movement of all objects, including changes in ownership, physical custody and curatorial assignment), events management, conservation management (recording all activities related to preparing objects for exhibit, loan, research and the long-term preservation of collections), publications management and information retrieval. The project is in the conceptual design stage, and the first terminals will be in place in late 1985 or early 1986. In addition to facilitating information management and retrieval for the staff, they will open the holdings of the Smithsonian to a new group of professional users outside the institution. In the not-too-distant future, some information will also be available to the visiting public through an English language vocabulary access to the system.

upgrade and enhance existing systems. The Museum of the American Indian in New York City, which has a collection of more than one million objects and artifacts, undertook computerization after the New York State attorney general ruled in 1976 that the museum must conduct a physical inventory. Midway through the manual process, an automated system was introduced. At first the museum was involved in a time-sharing system, but it now uses an in-house microcomputer for collections management, membership and development.

Museums should also be actively considering the documentation and research potential of videodiscs, which store both a visual image and catalog information. Some museums have begun to do so. The Horner Museum at Oregon State University has a videodisc catalog of its 2,400-object textile and clothing collection. At the Academy of Natural Sciences in Philadelphia, information about 1,000 specimens is stored in an easily accessible interactive videodisc format. And the National Air and Space Museum has produced an archival videodisc for research use, containing more than 100,000 images.

There must be more vigorous efforts by individual museums to join their colleagues that have moved into the technological age. Technologically sophisticated museums should actively share their expertise with smaller or less experienced institutions, in the interest of bringing the museum community as a whole up to date on the use of new information management technologies. The complex job of recording information about objects and making it accessible should, in most museums, eventually cease to be a wholly manual operation.

The Case for Research

Understanding, knowledge and appreciation—these are the ultimate goals of acquiring and caring for objects in museum collections. In the larger perspective the goal is, of course, to create a permanent record of human accomplishment and the natural world. Through exhibitions and scholarly activity, museums use their collections and strive to attain those goals. We will talk about exhibitions in the next chapter, when we examine the learning experience in museums. Since the care and organization of collections are so closely linked to research, particularly in museums of science and natural history, this is the logical place for a discussion of the range of scholarly pursuits undertaken to some degree in most museums.

"The case for research," said a museum director who attended a commission colloquium, "is the case for public understanding of our heritage." What we heard most clearly during the course of our work was an assertion of the significance of scholarly endeavor in the context of the museum, and serious concern that the research function is misunderstood and inadequately funded. Research has always been tacitly acknowledged as one of the most fundamental functions any museum performs, but it is clear that, as in the case of collections care, acknowledgment is not enough.

In any discussion of museum research, there are clear disciplinary lines. The research carried out by curators at the American Museum of Natural History bears little resemblance to the archeological research at Historic Annapolis or, for that matter, to research in preparation for an exhibition at the Houston Museum of Fine Arts. Despite the disciplinary differences, all museum research shares an orientation to objects. Were it not for research activity, the meaning of the objects, artifacts and specimens in museums would not be either understood or complete. Research brings museum collections to life, whether the goal is an exhibition for the public or an addition to a body of scholarly knowledge. Museum collections are vital sources of information that make possible a greater understanding of the principles of science, the creative genius of the artist, a way of life that no longer exists. Museums are the only places scholars can make comparisons and examine relationships between objects and concepts; as such, they are a rich potential source of new theories that may explain our increasingly complex existence.

In art museums, research is most often related to the development of exhibitions or publications; research is also done on conservation techniques. Until recently, with the establishment of the National Gallery of Art's Center for Advanced Study in the Visual Arts and the J. Paul Getty Trust's plans for a research institute, basic art historical research and publication have been the province of the academic community. In an effort to stimulate scholarly activity in art museums, the Luce

Community Museums

Many museums directly reflect the interests and efforts of their communities. That goes for minority museums in ethnic sections of large cities, historical societies in small towns and tribal organizations on Indian reservations. The Suquamish Tribal Cultural Center on the Fort Madison Indian Reservation in Suquamish, Washington, has worked for five years to reconstruct and preserve the history of the Suquamish Tribe. Its efforts culminated in the opening of a museum in June 1983.

The major challenge for those planning the Suquamish Museum was an accurate interpretation. They had to document the history and culture of the Suquamish people in the face of a historical record lacking both vital information and systematic interpretation and dominated by the perspective of non-Indian observers. The only immediate resource was the knowledge and memories of tribal elders, many of them in their 90s.

To accomplish this task, a photographic archives project set out to locate photographs relevant to Suquamish and Puget Sound Indian history. The more than 2,000 photographs that were found proved useful in stimulating the memories of tribal elders, who helped identify them.

As the photographic project advanced, an oral history component was added. The elders' recollections were recorded in a series of more than 150 tape-recorded and transcribed interviews. This material provided the basis for a language analysis program that generated, as an important by-product, strong community support. Regular luncheons brought together elders who lived at great distances. Some of them, recruited as VISTA volunteers, became community liaisons to ensure the continuing participation of others. Cooperating institutions have also used the photographic archive, and tribal oral history researchers have been paired with academic consultants in significant interchanges between the tribe and outsiders.

The entire Suquamish tribal community has been closely involved in the interpretation of exhibit and educational materials, guaranteeing a distinctly Indian perspective and offsetting distortions frequently found in the written record. A major exhibition, *The Eyes of Chief Seattle*, portrays the tribe's history and is tangible evidence for tribal members of their role in the region. The exhibition represented the city of Seattle at the inauguration of sister city relations with Nantes, France, and then returned to a permanent home as the opening exhibit for the Suquamish Museum.

The Suquamish Museum grew out of a community research effort. Occupying a major portion of the Suquamish Tribal Center, it is a vehicle for the presentation of the center's work. The center is the only institution in the region devoted exclusively to Puget Sound Salish Indians. It is also a "process," providing the basis for further research, collection development, and educational programs and a medium through which the tribe can sustain a dialogue with the non-Indian community.

Foundation now makes grants to enable museum staff to conduct concentrated research in American art.

Science and natural history museums, zoos and botanical gardens, as well as museums of anthropology and archeology, often conduct the most significant—and sometimes the only—research in certain fields of study. Large natural history museums, zoos and botanical gardens are centers of collections-based research with a serious responsibility for adding to the body of scientific knowledge. Research is so central to these museums that the collecting endeavor is driven by research needs; specimens are collected almost exclusively for research, which then makes possible the generalizations offered in exhibits for the public.

Research in these museums is often related to public needs, too, especially in matters affecting the environment and public health. At the request of Southern California Edison, the Natural History Museum of Los Angeles County is monitoring the effects of electrical generating activity on fish-breeding patterns off the California coast and bird migration patterns in the desert. Museums also prepare environmental impact statements and do work in forensic pathology.

Scholarly research in history museums is inseparable from exhibitions and public programs. Because history museums preserve the tangible evidence of civilizations, they are centers for archeological surveys and research in material culture, an endeavor that has recently gained respectability in the academic world. Sometimes large historical societies resemble natural history museums in that they are major research centers in which the scholarly function takes priority over public programming and exhibitions.

Since research in the museum context varies so much from discipline to discipline, it is difficult to generalize. There is, however, a common concern: scholarly activity in museums deserves greater understanding, prominence and support. In relation to that concern, there are three special issues we believe should be considered for the future.

The first concern is that museums must meet the research-related needs of their collections more effectively. Many of the concerns we have described elsewhere in this chapter—the need for carefully planned and coordinated growth of collections, a higher priority and adequate resources for their care, the implications of computer technologies—are concerns that affect the quality and priority of museum research. An active research program depends for its integrity on the growth and continuing reassessment of the collection. There can be no research without adequate documentation, and scholarly activity is greatly enhanced by the access computer technology can provide. In describing the critical needs we have introduced in this chapter, the museum profession must articulate an important end: to serve their full purpose, the objects in museums must be accessible to scholars, and for that to be possible, museum collections must be adequately maintained and properly documented. Grant-making agencies, both government and private, need to hear this message and make a stronger commitment to encouraging scholarly activity, particularly in smaller institutions where limited resources cause more visible functions to take priority.

Second, we believe both museums and the public would benefit from a closer relationship among the museum functions of research, exhibition and learning. Too often inflexible dichotomies separate research activity from public programs. At a time when fostering scientific understanding and visual appreciation is an important task for museums, research conducted by a museum's own curators can be a valuable resource for its exhibitions and programs. Using a collaborative approach to planning, curators, educators and designers can translate the product of scholarly work into exhibitions and programs for the visitor.

Finally, museum trustees, staff and supporters of museums must have a more complete understanding of the importance of research in the museum context. This understanding of the research function must then extend to the general public. Some museums are already introducing the research function to visitors through orientation galleries, special exhibits and publications. If the contributions of museums to society are to be recognized fully, public awareness of the process of research is as important as the product.

A Renewed Commitment to Collections Care

Cooperative Conservation Centers

In 1929 the Center for Conservation and Technical Studies at Harvard's Fogg Art Museum was founded to provide conservation education and treatment for museums and private collectors. Nearly 25 years later the Intermuseum Conservation Association was set up at Oberlin, Ohio, with a similar mission. These were the forerunners of the 11 cooperative conservation centers now located across the country. They include the Rocky Mountain Regional Conservation Center at the University of Denver, which specializes in the treatment of paintings, ethnographic objects, textiles and photographs, and the Conservation Center for Art and Historic Artifacts in Philadelphia, with its expertise in the treatment of paper. The centers serve primarily small and medium-sized museums that would never be able to maintain in-house conservation facilities. They also meet the conservation needs of historical societies, historic properties, universities and government agencies and even individual collectors.

In 1982 the 11 centers together served 1,224 clients. Of those, 415 were affiliated with member institutions, 216 were nonmember institutions and 593 were private collectors. The centers employ approximately 70 professional conservators, who treat objects and survey collections to identify needs. Most also provide educational services aimed at informing museum professionals about the conservation needs of the collections entrusted to their care. At the Center for Conservation and Technical Studies, for instance, a series of art conservation workshops for museum professionals other than conservators was instrumental in increasing awareness of collections needs and interest in securing adequate levels of care.

The success of these educational efforts has been a mixed blessing. With increased attention to conservation needs has come an increased demand for conservation services. The number of clients served by centers grows each year, but so does the amount of work. The backlogs, ranging from three months to one year, are so serious that one of the primary administrative concerns for the directors of centers is a policy for priority of treatment.

Financial stability is another concern for the future. The centers charge for their services, but they cannot recover all their expenses through fees. They should be expanding to meet increased demand for services, but equipment for conservation work is costly. The Williamstown Regional Art Conservation Center in Williamstown, Massachusetts, has been called on to treat more and more varied art objects that require additional equipment. For the first time in the center's history, the trustees have engaged a professional fund raiser to assist in their efforts. Other centers are developing multiyear fund-raising plans, and their directors are assuming major fund-raising responsibilities.

Together, the 11 cooperative conservation centers are an important element in the national effort to provide appropriate care of museum collections. In the fall of 1982, they formed the Association of Cooperative Conservation Centers to provide a forum for addressing common concerns and facilitate continued sharing of ideas.

In some respects the museum community has made significant progress in collections care, organization and research. The growing professional consciousness in museums involves a relatively new attention to activities related to the collections. The tasks associated with registration and conservation, for example, have greater prominence now than they did 15 years ago. They require specialized knowledge and skills and are often centralized in an individual or a department rather than dispersed among staff members. When asked to describe their museums' most important collections-related need, however, museum professionals still mention record keeping and conservation, both of which require human resources. This professional awareness puts museums in a good position to move to the next stage.

The tools are there. We have advanced technical knowledge about the conditions necessary to preserve objects of artistic, historic and scientific significance, although we need to learn more. Information management technology provides abundant opportunities for gathering, storing and retrieving data about collections. Funding is available, though not plentiful, and both public and private agencies have made some commitment to the care of museum collections.

Primarily, the museum community must strengthen its commitment to the organization and care of collections. This means there must be concerted efforts to acquire and organize information about the quantity and location of objects, assess and make known the maintenance and preservation needs of collections, strengthen institutional commitment to collections care and maintenance, and promote an understanding of the critical needs of collections among policy makers, funding sources and the public.

A related task is to provide internal incentives that stimulate the renewal of commitment. To its credit, the museum community has always recognized the importance of self-developed standards, so the mechanism for these incentives is already in place. The AAM's Accreditation Program, for example, should continue to insist on the highest standards for the care of collections. Museums must impose similarly high standards on one another when objects are loaned, exhibitions circulated or collections used for scholarly research.

Trustees and staff—even those who have no direct involvement with objects—must be more knowledgeable about the basic principles of care and maintenance. It is as important for a trustee or a public relations director to know about the collection's vital needs as it is for a conservator to keep abreast of the latest advances in techniques. Arthur Beale, director of the Center for Conservation and Technical Studies at Harvard's Fogg Art Museum, attests to the value of the center's art conservation workshops for museum professionals other than conservators. It has been, he says, the single most important thing the center has done to promote commitment to the principles of good collections care.

Finally, we believe small and developing museums need more technical assistance in all aspects of collections management. Basic information must be made available through existing and new programs sponsored by museum service organizations, public agencies or museums themselves, so the staffs and volunteers of smaller institutions recognize all aspects of good collections management and feel equipped to assess the problems of their own collections and move toward adequate solutions.

♦ RECOMMENDATION 4: The lack of information about the number, location and condition of objects, artifacts and specimens in the nation's museums is a handicap to adequate care and maintenance of these collections and to scholarly progress in general. We urge a planning study to determine the feasibility of a national series of inventories of museum collections, organized and conducted by discipline. These inventories will be the basis for sound future collections management as well as for the development of sound collections policies. The various museum service organizations should collaborate in the planning study.

In addition to proposing a mechanism for carrying out inventories, the study should initiate the development of an information-sharing system for all museums that could eventually include data about acquisition and disposal of objects; research activities; the use of collections by educational institutions, print and broadcast media; and sharing museum collections through loans and exhibitions.

3 A New Imperative for Learning

Ours is a society with tremendous hopes and expectations for education. It is perhaps a fundamental sign of American optimism that we have such a stake in what Thomas Jefferson called the "crusade against ignorance." Education in this country—and we use the word broadly to describe the development of knowledge, skills and character—is a pillar of democracy, a mediator for social, economic and intellectual opportunity. We depend on education to help us compensate for deficiencies and circumvent crises. We want our educational system to make available to all of us the full complement of advantages a civilized society can offer.

Museums have long been participants in this national crusade. In fact, many consider public education to be the most significant contribution this country has made to the evolution of the museum concept. In Europe the first museums were established to preserve royal collections; in America they were often founded with the notion of public education clearly in mind. Long before the Tax Reform Act of 1969 officially designated museums as educational institutions, American museums embraced the notion that they should communicate the essence of ideas, impart knowledge, encourage curiosity and promote esthetic sensibility. If collections are the heart of museums, what we have come to call education—the commitment to presenting objects and ideas in an informative and stimulating way—is the spirit.

Since the early part of this century, educators and scholars have written about the educational responsibilities of museums. Benjamin Ives Gilman, Henry Watson Kent and John Cotton Dana are all familiar names in museum history. Although Gilman advocated esthetic sensitivity rather than education per se as the most important function of a museum, he is considered to have invented the principle of gallery instruction at the Museum of Fine Arts, Boston, in the first part of this century. Kent, who worked at the Metropolitan Museum of Art in the same era, was a champion of the idea that museums must touch a broad variety of people through, among other things, the establishment of branches. In this way, he was an early proponent of the principle of outreach. The director of the Newark Museum from 1909 to 1929, Dana was one of the most passionate promulgators of museums as institutions of learning. He believed education was a museum's social responsibility and should be its primary mission.

True to Dana's philosophy, some museums were founded with learning as their primary mission. Science-technology centers are dedicated to the education of children and adults alike, and they have been pioneers in the development of experiential methods and "hands-on" exhibits. Children's museums seek to introduce children and their families to the world around them. Their exemplary educational programs grow out of a substantial commitment of both effort and resources.

But in all museums the impulse toward education of the public is strong. Exhibitions involve a great deal more than the mere display of objects, artifacts or specimens. Gallery labels not only identify but explain. Brochures and catalogs tell the larger story of the materials on view and put them in context. Docents give gallery talks; curators give lectures. Special tours are arranged for schoolchildren. Computerized interpretation devices enable visitors to be actively involved in the displays. The American museum does not simply exhibit; it teaches as well.

In the past 20 years or so, the variety of programs that support the educational component of

museums has grown, as museums have enjoyed greater popularity and acknowledge more fully their role as public service institutions. An aspect of the museum movement, as we have described it, is the public's increased enthusiasm for informal learning. Generally higher levels of formal education and stronger personal commitment to lifelong learning have prompted people to want more from museums; they visit museums to learn.

Museums have both helped create this general public enthusiasm and responded to it by seeking out the patterns of public interest. They are trying to be accessible to the physically handicapped and convenient to public parking and transportation. Increasingly, they are going to people by train, in airports, through live performances, in shopping malls. In Michigan, Artrain takes exhibits from town to town; in 1983, 12 communities saw *Creative Impulse*, and hundreds of schools participated in an accompanying program that prepared students for the Artrain experience. Travelers passing through San Francisco International Airport are treated to a museum "visit." With technical assistance from the Fine Arts Museums of San Francisco, the Airport Commission has sponsored changing art exhibitions that make the airport environment more welcoming and promote the cultural life of the Bay Area. In Baltimore a group of museums—the USS *Constellation*, the Carroll Mansion and the Museum of Industry—use theater to bring history to life. "History is not a book gathering dust," announces the promotional material of the Living Legends Program. In a number of cities, the Rouse Company's Art in the Marketplace Program brings museum exhibits to shopping malls.

There is an ancient tradition for all this, as Joel N. Bloom, director of the Franklin Institute Science Museum and Planetarium in Philadelphia, reminds us:

> The muses were beloved for coming down from the temple, bearing their gifts of dance and poetry. They moved through the bustling streets . . . with the stuff of spiritual life, inspiring the people. In some respects, we have since captured them and put them back in the temple, that house of refuge we call a museum. But the business of . . . outreach programs has been to return the museum to our modern streets, to the shopping centers and other areas of activity where people can be found today.

Despite the obvious commitment of museums to learning, there is still confusion in the public mind about the role of museums as educational institutions and, within the museum world, about the role of education in the institutional structure. Willard L. Boyd, president of the Field Museum of Natural History in Chicago, describes the problem well. People understand institutions of formal education, he says, because virtually everyone is exposed to them as a student, a parent or, in later life, an alumnus. The public's exposure to cultural institutions, on the other hand, is "episodic, and more diverse. . . . The American public tends to think that cultural institutions only enrich. [But they] do more than enrich; they strengthen basic skills, basic knowledge, basic comprehension, and basic understanding. Cultural institutions educate, and each year educate more and more people."

Frank Oppenheimer, director of the Exploratorium in San Francisco, expresses surprise at the dichotomies people draw between formal and informal education. "The whole point of education," he says, "is to transmit culture, and museums can play an increasingly important role in this process. It is a mistake to think that preserving culture is distinct from transmitting it through education."

As this commission first began to consider the matter of museum learning for a new century, we knew we faced a particular challenge. Educational responsibility is firmly imbedded in the philosophical foundation of museums, but there is no clear understanding of how people can learn best in the museum environment—a situation that is ironic when one considers the quantity and the quality of educational programming in museums today. Confusion over the learning function of museums stems in part from the failure of museum professionals to articulate, to the satisfaction of all involved, the nature of the learning experience. Although museums are plainly institutions of object-centered learning and there is interest among educators and administrators alike in formulating museum learning theory more clearly, there is no accepted philosophical framework. Discussions invariably focus on the nuts and bolts of programming—on specific activities, materials and methods. These practical matters are important, but not as important as exploring issues that define learning in the museum context.

The absence of consensus about learning in museums stems also from a paradox of significant proportions, a tension of values that is inherent in

Two Decades of Outreach

In 1972, a special study committee of the American Association of Museums concluded in *Museums: Their New Audiences*: "There is a crisis in the world of the American museum. . . . The museum as an institution is a city institution. The city in America has changed profoundly over the last generation. . . . The focusing of museum interest upon the obligation and opportunity to assist the new urban community is the most urgent and important task facing the museum now." The report went on to make recommendations and provide examples of 16 programs geared toward attracting and serving new audiences.

Twelve years later, museums still seek to be involved in their communities, but their approach to minority people and cultures has changed. As James Elliott, who cochaired the study committee, recently reflected, museums in the 1960s were "concerned with making the museum physically as well as psychologically available." Outreach programs were designed to bring museums directly to people who were not otherwise likely to visit them.

Today, outreach has come to mean community involvement *inside* the museum. When this commission surveyed the 16 programs profiled in the earlier report, one trend was strikingly evident: outreach efforts of the 1960s and 1970s that were carried on outside the museum are now either housed within the museum or no longer exist. The New Thing Art and Architecture Center in Washington, D.C., for example, once sponsored workshops in media and the visual arts. Located in a renovated house, the center was affiliated with the Corcoran Gallery of Art and the Smithsonian Institution, but neither museum linked the center's activities to its regular programming. Today it is gone.

The same pattern is evident in other parts of the country. Neighborhood Arts, once in an inner-city neighborhood and sponsored by the Akron Art Museum, no longer exists. Other outreach programs were difficult or impossible to find because their personnel, location and nature had changed. People affiliated with them were usually not museum professionals, and most have not entered the profession.

Among those programs still in existence, the trend has been toward expanding services. At the Walker Art Center in Minneapolis, for instance, programs for new audiences have continued, and support from staff and board members has grown. The Virginia Museum of Fine Arts reports that its outreach programs—affiliate chapters throughout the state that bring the museum's resources to Virginians who don't live in Richmond—are more professional. The New Muse Community Museum of Brooklyn, once called MUSE and known as an arm of the Brooklyn Children's Museum, has changed its focus, not its audience. The director, Jackie Woods, says, "We play a role in the community that is no different from any other museum in New York. We exist to preserve items that have significance to African heritage."

In the past decade outreach programs have discontinued social services and strengthened ties to the collection and mission of museums. Speculating on future directions, Elliott reflected that the public perception of museums has changed significantly in the last 25 years. What's new is the belief that not everyone should or has to visit museums. But museums have an obligation: "Every effort should be made to publicize and facilitate the visit—that's what these new outreach programs are all about." As museums focus on helping new audiences to have quality visits, the effort might more logically be called "inreach."

the very mission of museums. Stated quite simply, the concerns of preservation and the demands of public access are a contradiction lived out in every institution. Gary Esolen, a New Orleans writer and editor, talked about the dilemma during one of our open forums. Museums, he said,

> should be places that both conserve and display objects, places where the public comes to learn and where the staff can also learn and grow, places that are easily accessible to outsiders and still hold special treasures for insiders. These things can coexist, but one will try to crowd out the other, and only a perpetual wariness will hold the complex mixture intact.

It was a conscious and purposeful decision of this commission to speak of "learning" rather than "education" in an effort to change the character of the discussion. We want to stimulate talk about the museum as a place of learning. By diverting attention from the specifics of programs and materials, staffs and budgets, we want to encourage museum professionals to see learning as a museumwide endeavor. Only then will learning be fully integrated with the other responsibilities of museums and the role of museums as educational institutions in service to society be clarified.

What is learning in the museum setting? Museums are agents of visual, scientific and historical literacy. They have stewardship for the objects that show the progression of human existence, the creative energy of civilizations and the phenomena of science, nature and technology. Museums preserve and display "the real thing." These objects are the basis of the museum experience and the root of a museum's educational potential.

Learning in a museum is studying the work of the French impressionists in the original. It is seeing the chair in which Lincoln was shot. It is finding out about the principle of combustion by watching it happen in a live demonstration. It is understanding hearing impairment by experiencing a world of diminished sound through earphones. It is wandering among sculpture or through period rooms and discovering something new each time.

In museums, the individual human experience can find a cultural context, a place in time and space. To "learn" in a museum means to develop the ability to synthesize ideas and form opinions, shape an esthetic and cultural sensibility. These intellectual qualities result from all kinds of learning, but they are the special province of museums, where objects and ideas are interwoven in an open process of communication that blends study and exploration, seeing and thinking and, in many instances, touching.

Anthropologist Nelson H. H. Graburn sees in museum learning the potential to build cultural self-confidence and bridge the barriers of class and ethnicity. In addition to preserving and presenting the whole of human heritage, museums promote what he calls the "symbolic estate"—a personal view of that heritage. If museums fail to encourage the many "symbolic estates" of their audience, they become "backwaters or attics, collecting the cast-offs of others." The late Joshua Taylor once lamented the popular perception of the museum as "a kind of beachhead with no life of its own." A museum, he said, "is a bridge that should be well-traveled."

Boston Children's Museum director Michael Spock describes what happens in museums as "landmark learning." Although every part of a museum will not have a profound effect on everyone, each visitor is likely to be moved in a special way by something he or she sees. That becomes a "landmark" in the visitor's lifelong learning experience.

Every visitor brings a distinct set of experiences, interests and motives to the museum. Most do not approach museum collections or special exhibitions intent on gaining a particular bit of information, but that only makes learning in museums education in the broadest sense. The goal is to stimulate the innate desire to learn, to expand one's horizons. Learning in museums is a spontaneous, individualized process; it cannot be imposed on the visitor. When museum education emphasizes teaching and verbal communication, it does a disservice to the museum as a learning environment.

Museums have yet to realize their full potential as educational institutions. We believe a new approach to learning in museums must be developed, one that does justice to the unique learning environment they provide. Both inside and outside museums, the opportunities for fresh vision and a clearer consensus on museum learning are there. Trends in education in this country, the trusted position museums have as independent institutions with intellectual authority and the fact that many are models of educational excellence all bode well for the future.

The Nature of the Museum Experience

Museums provide a learning environment and incentives fundamentally different from those provided by schools. These differences produce different effects. Museums stimulate the imagination, sharpen powers of observation and enrich thinking. They encourage an appreciation of other cultures, other times, other world views, of animal and plant life and artistic expression. They more directly involve the visitor.

Those who have studied the effects of the museum visit agree that the museum experience is individual and personal. The learning that takes place involves not only the command of new information but an increased understanding of one's self, one's relationship to others and to the world in general.

Nelson H. H. Graburn, professor of anthropology at the University of California, Berkeley, has described a "revolution of rising expectations" in what people want from cultural institutions. For many reasons, museums today are more popular than ever; attendance alone attests to that. But their importance cannot be measured in attendance figures. It is in elevating awareness—esthetic, historical, scientific and humanistic—that museums serve human needs, a benefit that cannot be quantified but must be recognized. Graburn has identified three human needs that the museum can fulfill.

■ *The reverential experience.* There is a universal human need for a personal experience with something higher, purer or more eternal, more possessed of authority, more extraordinary than home, work and the everyday world can afford us. For many people, the museum—though a public space—provides an experience that is solitary, contemplative, a rest from the cares of the world, an uplifting of the spirit. For these visitors, the museum is a place of peace and fantasy, a place to be alone with one's thoughts amid objects that are beautiful, that inspire, that one loves.

■ *An associational space.* For other visitors, the museum is attractive because it is the focus of a social occasion; it offers an experience that can be shared. Families, couples and friends come together, and they spend more time relating to each other than to the objects on display. To fulfill this social role, the museum must be comfortable, with seating areas and access to social space for a variety of personal interactions. For these people, museum visits are pleasurable group outings.

■ *The educational function.* It is the educational function of the museum that appeals to visitors seeking to make sense of their world. Museums offer broader continuing education than do schools. They convey information, but they are far more than "three-dimensional textbooks," for they stimulate translation of the original into the context of personal values. As Graburn puts it, "The museum is a stage on which a production is presented which allows the visitor the freedom of movement, thought and timing to interpret the objects in his or her own familiar terms."

Each of us may be, in different times and moods, any one of these types of museum visitors. The point is that museums provide a variety of experiences that fulfill a spectrum of human needs and that are not, in quite the same way, available anywhere else.

This commission seeks to lead the field in reaching a consensus about the nature of learning in museums. There are a number of steps in the task:

- A reexamination of the educational function in the internal structure of museums;
- A serious consideration of the power of the exhibition as a medium of communication and learning;
- A stronger commitment to research into the distinctive character of museum learning and the potential of electronic technology in educational programming;
- A new definition of the relationship between museums and schools;
- A clearer recognition of the special responsibilities museums have to adults, who will constitute a higher proportion of the museum audience in the future.

Learning within the Museum Structure

With the increasing emphasis on the educational role of museums has come the formation of internal departments assigned the primary responsibility for planning and carrying out the variety of activities that fall under the umbrella of "education." These are the programs that teach—that develop activities, in conjunction with exhibitions, for schoolchildren and special audiences, that supervise and train the docents who give tours and gallery talks and, at historic sites, serve as costumed guides and interpreters. The practitioners of museum education are often specialists in teaching. Meanwhile the curators, with academic degrees in art history, history and the scientific fields related to the museum's disciplines, continue to write the gallery labels and the exhibition catalogs and, by and large, deliver the lectures.

There is, on the one hand, an increasing professionalism about museum education. At the same time there is an increasing separation of the public programs museum educators develop from the academic work of the institution. While it was once seen as an encouraging sign, there are indications now that the proliferation of departments designed specifically to plan and carry out the museum's educational programs can have a deleterious side effect—the intellectual isolation of the learning function from exhibitions, research and other museum activities with which it should be inextricably joined. This is one dilemma museums have to face.

Within the administrative structure of museums, education is often perceived as an adjunct function, and thus it is vulnerable to budget cuts when other needs seem more pressing. Museum education is sometimes so narrowly defined that its practical application is limited to programs for schoolchildren, and its usefulness to the whole museum is seen from the same perspective. The image of the education department can be further colored by its close association with volunteers, who usually work under its auspices. Their contributions to the museum are undeniable, but the juxtaposition of paid and unpaid staff, with separate motivations and interests, can create tension. Many museum educators, though they have achieved a stronger sense of professional confidence in recent decades, still feel caught between two worlds, outside the mainstream of both museum work and the field of education. With this kind of intellectual isolation, the quality of the programs they offer can only suffer.

What is most important is that the museum's educational function be an integral part of all museum activities. From scholarly research to public relations, the museum's educational purpose must never be lost sight of. If learning is to remain at the philosophical core of museums, we believe its place in the internal structure of museums must be reexamined. Placing all educational efforts under the director of a separate department may not be the best organizational structure for achieving the museum's educational goals.

Some museums have begun to experiment with new organizational structures that break away from assigning "separate but equal" status to various museum functions. A new model groups staff in four divisions—collections, programs, finance and public affairs—the programs division encompassing specialists in exhibit design, education and publications, who work together in planning activities for the public. At some museums, a deputy or associate director of all "nonoperation" functions is assigned responsibility for education. An example is the newly reorganized Milwaukee Public Museum, which has only two divisions—programs and operations—each headed by a deputy director. This system was initiated to encour-

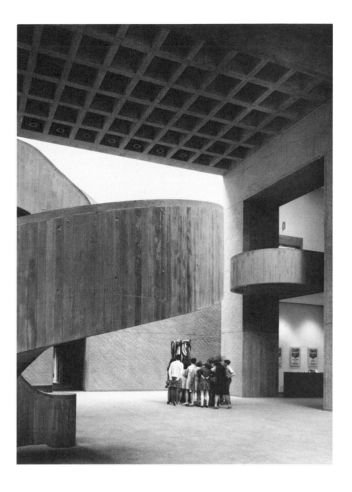

Computers and Educational Programming

In 1982 the National Audio-Visual Association (NAVA) presented its Award of Excellence to the U.S. Department of Commerce for innovative use of audiovisual communications media in the U.S. pavilion at the Knoxville World's Fair. As NAVA executive vice-president Harry McGee commented, "If ever an event did a better job of introducing the general public to new communications technologies and their implications, it could only have been the 1939 World's Fair, where many people saw television for the first time. Now, at the 1982 World's Fair, you have been giving visitors a taste of the dramatic effect that video and computer technology will have on their lives in the not-too-distant future."

For the exhibit, designers at Ramirez & Woods in New York City relied heavily on microcomputer technology—most notably computer-driven interactive videodiscs—to tell the story of the nation's energy sources, uses and outlooks. At six video stations visitors could call up text, slides or motion picture presentations that explained any one of 480 energy terms that crossed the screen. When the definition appeared, viewers could ask for additional information by touching specific words on the screen. They could learn what they wanted in as much or as little detail as desired.

A major attraction of new communications technology is the ability to offer one-on-one communication between the user and program; the storage capacity of computers means users have ready access to large quantities of information. The responsiveness of the technology makes it well suited to applications in museums, where the goals are educational and the audience diverse.

Science-technology centers were the first to introduce computers to museum exhibits, and for many visitors places like the Lawrence Hall of Science in Berkeley are nearly synonymous with computer simulations and games. But museums of all types are now beginning to use computers in their exhibit halls. With recent advances in technology and increased public curiosity about the interpretive contributions computers can make, a number of exemplary programs have been developed.

▪ *Orientation.* The formidable task of choosing among New York City's many cultural exhibits is now made easy thanks to a new computerized information service available free of charge at the IBM Gallery of Science and Art. The NYCulture Guide lets visitors inquire about more than 200 museums, exhibition spaces, historic sites, zoos and botanical gardens in all five boroughs. By simply touching a color video screen, users can find the attractions that best suit their interests, schedule, itinerary and budget. The information can be called up by the name of the institution, its location or its subject area or specialty. A person can, for example, ask for a list of every public institution in the city with a work of art by Picasso.

▪ *Computer games.* In an attempt to demonstrate that arcade-style video games can indeed be educational, Philadelphia's Franklin Institute Science Museum has created an entire room of fun-to-play, flashy games that teach science lessons. Rather than perfecting sharp-shooting skills, as typical video games do, the games employ an understanding of principles of momentum, geometry and wind, subjects that are explained in more traditional exhibits in the museum. "Rocket Mail" challenges the player to launch a rocket over a mountain to a target just past a village. The player must guess the angle of ascent and the amount of fuel required, taking into account wind velocity and the rocket's weight.

To provide exhibits that are both fun and educational, the Erie County Historical Society Museum in Pennsylvania developed a series of computer games. "Victorian Architecture in Erie" displays a map of the historic area of Erie. Visitors are introduced to three distinctly different architectural styles and invited to rebuild a house by adding appropriate doors, windows, materials and special features such as towers and gingerbread work. "Rags to Riches: A Game of 1890s Economics" presents players with information about the assets and liabilities of four businesses at different times in Erie history. Players begin with $5,000 and make investment decisions. Successful investors see their companies prosper. The object of the game is to study balance sheets, think about historical events and invest wisely.

▪ *Computer centers.* The Capital Children's Museum in Washington, D.C., operates the Future Center complete with a computer curriculum. On weekdays school and other groups come to the center for classes in computer languages like BASIC and LOGO. The center also offers a graduate-level computer course for the U.S. Department of Agriculture's continuing education program. On weekends the center is open to the general public. Under supervision, visitors can use its software library to play games, learn from educational packages or operate word processing programs.

▪ *Simulations.* The Brooklyn Museum added a technological dimension to *The Great East River Bridge* through the use of a computer simulation. Prepared as part of the Brooklyn Bridge centennial, the exhibit included paintings, drawings and photographs of the bridge from the time of its construction until 1983. Its highlight, however, was a collection of original drawings by John Roebling, the engineer who designed the bridge, and the museum wanted visitors to understand some of the technical aspects of the drawings and the bridge's construction. Museum curators worked with the Computer Review Center, a computer design firm, to develop six separate programs. One gave a history of the bridge; the others each focused on an aspect of the bridge's construction—anchorage, caissons, towers, suspension and the roadway. In explaining the construction, the computer programs featured art work of such a high quality that some visitors saw it as still another artistic rendering of the bridge.

At the Impression 5 Museum in Lansing, Michigan, computers teach visitors about the scientific method and the principles of mechanics in an exhibit called *Playground Physics*. A swing explains the operation of pendulums; a slide demonstrates the material properties of falling objects of various sizes, weights and materials. The computer summarizes information about the principles involved, initiates the experiments and lets visitors know if their hypotheses are correct.

New technologies hold as much promise for learning in museums as they do for fiscal and collections management. Pilot projects indicate that, with careful planning, equipment can be tailored for use by large crowds, quality images can be achieved and a wide variety of visitor interests can be satisfied. The combination of computers and video is certain to make museums even more exciting centers of informal learning in the future.

age better coordination between the collections-related functions of the museum and its public programs.

The operating assumption in these new organizational structures is the importance of public programs as museumwide activities, not as a series of isolated functions. Everything that occurs in these museums to show and interpret the collections to the public or create and promote the museum's image is considered part of the museum's educational function.

A new approach to the place of education in the functioning of museums is a matter not only for individual institutions. Working together with museums, universities and organizations that provide graduate or continuing education programs in museum administration should explore new managerial options, including a new place for museum education. Graduate training in the academic disciplines leading to museum work should stress the educational function of museums, so prospective curators have a full understanding of the public side of their responsibilities.

◆ RECOMMENDATION 5: Education is a primary purpose of American museums. To assure that the educational function is integrated into all museum activities, museums need to look carefully at their internal operational structures. Collaborative approaches to public programs that include educational as well as scholarly and exhibition components facilitate achieving the full educational mission of museums.

The Power of the Exhibition

Any reconsideration of museum learning must include the exhibition—the museum's primary means of communication and a medium so powerful that it can be the most prominent aspect of a museum's public face. As we appeal to people to use museums as learning resources, the force of the exhibition as an instrument of learning must be acknowledged. And as the public sees museums more clearly as institutions of authority and social responsibility, the exhibition's power to convey a message is worth careful attention.

Historian Neil Harris, who joined commission members at our colloquium on the museum in society, describes the responsibility of museums to offer exhibitions that stimulate the visitor to form a point of view: "To insist that a museum bar advocacy from its exhibitions would be insisting that a university bar argument from its classrooms: unthinkable not simply because [it would] interfere with a statement of opinion, but because it inhibits thought and constrains experience."

The exhibition is such a powerful medium because its message is sponsored by an institution of perceived authority. Just as learning is an essential element in the museum experience, so the communication of a point of view is an inevitable component in an exhibition. The "advocacy" Neil Harris describes is not the promulgation of a political or ethical position but the responsible stimulation of ideas and opinions. *Can Man Survive?*, the exhibition on population growth at the American Museum of Natural History in the late 1960s, was an exhibition with a message. So was the Mount Holyoke College Art Museum's recent exhibition of artists' renditions of nuclear war. So is a period room, a retrospective of an artist's work or an exhibition about a scientific principle. The potential power of the exhibition requires that the medium be used responsibly, with full recognition of the museum's intellectual independence, its integrity and authority as an institution and the obligations inherent in its public educational role.

Research about Museum Learning

Visitors to museums have been the subject of occasional study since the late 1920s, with most research focusing on demographic profiles, the effects of visitor orientation, seasonal visiting patterns and time-motion studies of visitor behavior. Recently, attention has shifted to the measurable impact of a museum visit, from the effect of participatory exhibits in science museums to the effect of videotapes associated with an art museum's collection. Even this research, however, focuses on adjuncts to an exhibition—self-guides, docent presentations and audio tours—rather than on the exhibition itself. There has been little research on object-centered learning or the nature of the museum experience.

Museum exhibits are object-based, visual and spatial. They engender a kind of learning very different from that prompted by the printed page or formal lecture. In the past, studies of learning in the museum setting have employed measures intended for schools, and they proved inappropriate. It was not altogether surprising to discover that, when these measures were used, museum exhibits and programs seemed to produce very little change in level of knowledge.

In order to understand the dimensions of museum learning, new procedures and instruments are needed that go beyond those developed for the classroom or the lecture hall. If we are truly committed to the idea that museums are more than passive repositories of objects and that museum learning is unique and important, we must study the special nature of learning in museums on its own terms.

There is little agreement among museum professionals about what in fact constitutes an effective exhibit. Empirical research is needed to guide debate. Information is needed about visitors' responses to variations in color, lighting and labeling, size, number, complexity and placement of objects, and the dynamics of visual and interactive learning. Further, comparative data are needed to differentiate the general principles of exhibition techniques from the effects of specific museum contexts.

The use of electronic technology in museum education is another area that merits research. Computer and video technology, which is becoming more and more affordable for museum use, can link visitors to collections and exhibits in a highly personal way, adding a new dimension to learning in the museum context. Video tapes and discs, computer-video linkages and holography all present opportunities to enhance museum learning. Although methods of computer-assisted instruction developed for the classroom could be adapted for museums, approaches tailored to museums are needed. The heterogeneity of the museum audience, the absence of standard curricula and the unique self-structured nature of the museum experience all dictate the development of special instructional programs and strategies.

Research in museums, as in other field settings, is challenging. It is difficult to go beyond what is easily accessible, to measure what a museum exhibit or program is attempting to accomplish. It is difficult to maintain experimental control and yet not alter the visitor's behavior or detract from the museum experience. The great diversity of exhibits makes it difficult to generalize research findings even within a single institution. Both theoretically and empirically, the development of research tools for investigating museum learning is in its infancy. Finally, it is difficult to translate

Evaluation Research

Thousands of research studies (sometimes referred to as audience research studies) have been conducted in museums over the past 60 years. The efforts began with a series of pioneering studies of visitor behavior in 1925 when the American Association of Museums received a grant from the Carnegie Corporation for research on museum fatigue under the direction of Edward S. Robinson, professor of psychology at Yale. As part of the series, Marguerite Bloomberg investigated the differential effects of various ways of preparing schoolchildren for museum visits. Studying fifth-grade children of different intelligence levels at the Cleveland Museum of Art, she concluded that the best format included a previsit lesson and the formation of questions by the students themselves. Her 1929 monograph remains a fine example of sound methodology employed to examine elements of museum-school programs.

After those early studies there was very little research on the interaction between visitors and museum programs until the 1960s, when Chandler Screven, a psychologist at the University of Wisconsin—Milwaukee, began exploring strategies to increase learning in the museum setting. Screven worked with a classic experimental model to measure visitor reactions to exhibits. He is best known for his studies on how principles of instructional design and human motivation might be helpful in facilitating learning in the museum. Most important are his findings about specifying learning outcomes, breaking exhibit content into instructional elements and providing some kind of visitor interaction that allows for responses and feedback. A few museums, such as the Science Museum of Virginia in Richmond, the National Museum of American History and the Denver Art Museum, use results from audience studies like Screven's in their exhibit and program planning.

The greatest challenge facing museum researchers has been developing measures appropriate to the museum setting. In fact, one major study conducted by Minda Borun at the Franklin Institute Science Museum in Philadelphia was titled *Measuring the Immeasurable*. Borun resolved some of the difficulties in her own research by recognizing the personal dimension to learning in the museum. She consistently assesses both the cognitive and affective components of the museum experience. In her most recent effort—a collaboration with the Museum of Science in Boston—Borun developed visual measures which confirm that schoolchildren increase their knowledge of science content during a museum visit. Skepticism about the ability of researchers to represent the true nature of the museum experience have been allayed in similar studies that identify the variability in the museum audience, allow for multiple experiences and outcomes and develop measures that respond to the visual as well as the verbal aspects of museum visits. The best results are obtained when a trained researcher works closely with members of the museum staff.

Though audience research is not new, it is just now being recognized by museum professionals for its value in exhibit planning and design. As more museums discover the benefits of evaluation research, the body of information about learning in museums is bound to increase, and with it the quality of museum exhibits and programs.

research findings into information that can be used by museum professionals. Nevertheless, if museums are to be effective centers of informal learning, they must have an objective means of evaluating their efforts and determining where improvements are needed.

In order to answer basic questions, serious, systematic investigation of the process of learning in museums must be carried out. This requires that consistent units of measurement and instruments of data collection be developed. Research tools and methods must reflect the differences between the museum and other, more formal learning environments. They must yield valid and reliable measures of learning that can serve as the basis for informed decisions.

◆ RECOMMENDATION 6: We urge a high priority for research into the ways people learn in museums. Continuing, systematic research into these unique processes and mechanisms is the key to the success of the museum as an environment for learning. Research is also needed to guide the introduction of computers and other electronic technology into museum learning. Universities linked with consortiums of museums in particular fields might provide a mechanism for implementing these studies.

The Museum-School Partnership

Elsewhere in this report we speak of the need for collaboration among museums and between museums and other cultural and educational institutions. The collaborative spirit is nowhere more evident than in the museum-school partnership, perhaps the most longstanding and successful example of the interest and ability of museums to join forces with other institutions in working toward common goals.

Programs for schoolchildren are the most frequent educational offering of museums. Informal surveys indicate that twice as many visits to museums are made by schoolchildren as by other members of the public. Guided tours, in-school presentations by museum staff or volunteers and school loan services are available in more than half the nation's museums. Most people first visit a museum as youngsters with a school group, and those experiences have a profound effect on their attitude toward museums.

But museums are not simply adjuncts to the classroom. The report of the Commission on the Humanities explains why: "Facts must be shown to have a living use, or they may deaden a young mind." Museums add a tangible, familiar dimension to the learning that takes place in a formal setting. Studying the brush strokes and true colors on a canvas, watching an animal's behavior in its own environment, seeing how a family once lived in a historic house or re-creating important scientific experiments—these are the experiences museums can provide. They also demonstrate that the spirit of inquiry is not limited to the classroom but a value permeating American society at large. Again and again, museums have shown that their partnership with schools helps complete—not just enrich—the process of enlivening young minds.

The long relationship between museums and schools has been marked not only by success but by dissatisfaction and frustration. Logistical shortcomings are sometimes at fault, but the relationships among institutions can vary so much that it is difficult to generalize. For the purposes of this report, we would prefer to speak of a more fundamental issue that does not change from situation to situation: communication among museum educators, schoolteachers and administrators about their mutual objectives and about the quality of the experience they together offer schoolchildren.

As a commission composed primarily of museum professionals, we confess that we approached this subject from the museum side of the partnership. We had heard museum educators express frustration that teachers think museums are little more than a convenient respite from classroom routine. Most programs are aimed at elementary school audiences. When the curriculum gets "serious" in high school, museum visits are hard to coordinate with class schedules, and most high school students have little organized exposure to museums. Programs in which the museum experience is a consistent, fully integrated part of the formal school curriculum are few and far between. Where museum programs are used to enrich the curriculum, they are shaped by the needs of the schools, not the strengths of the museum. The museum experience seems auxiliary, and museum educators feel constricted by the limits they feel the schools establish.

Martin Deeks recently studied museum-school collaborations, and his findings bear out these impressions. Only 9 of the 23 programs he exam-

The Educational Role of the Museum

This commission has asserted that museums make a major contribution to education, so it is heartening to know that similar commissions in the humanities and in education have also recognized the significant role museums can play. *The Humanities in American Life*, the 1980 report of the Commission on the Humanities, asks museums to explain more about the context of the objects they display and to share their collections to increase public access. It also calls for increased federal and private support for museum operations and special projects. The specific recommendations are:

▪ Museums should mount more exhibits informing visitors of the cultural, esthetic, historical and technical forces surrounding the creating of the objects displayed. More use of permanent collections and more sharing of collections among institutions would increase public access to our national treasury of historical and cultural artifacts.

▪ Federal support for general operating expenses of museums should expand through increased appropriations not only for the Institute of Museum Services and the Challenge Grant Programs of both endowments, but also for grants from the NEH, NEA and National Science Foundation; private sources of support should provide more funds for general operating expenses.

Educating Americans for the 21st Century, issued in 1983 by the National Science Board Commission on Precollege Education in Mathematics, Science and Technology, applauds the educational efforts of science museums and commends their ability to entertain while educating. It calls on science museums to increase their science teacher training activities and urges that both private sector and federal funds support them. The commission specifically recommends:

▪ Science museums should serve as a focus for community interest in informal learning about science and technology. Science museums, whenever possible, should offer a full range of activities and opportunities to pursue science hobbies, teacher-training programs, weekend and evening programs for parents and children, and opportunities for "hands-on" experience to complement the stimulus and background experience provided by television and reading.

▪ The federal government should provide supplementary support for museum education activities in mathematics, science and technology at a level that will encourge a rich spectrum of activities and options.

▪ Local business groups should work with museums to encourage, support and publicize their education activities.

Recognizing the financial ramifications of these recommendations, the National Science Board Commission calls on the federal government to allocate $25 million for the museum education activities described in the recommendation.

ined were truly joint efforts; the rest were initiated by museums. Again, only 9 of the 23 consisted of more than a single visit or event.

During our open forums and our colloquium on education, we heard the other side of the story, as school administrators and educators expressed parallel frustrations. "You don't let us know what you have to offer," a science curriculum planner said. "How can we give our teachers and students the full benefit of the museum experience if you don't tell us what museums can contribute?" At first glance this remark identifies one of the barriers to successful partnerships; at second glance, it may indicate the solution.

We believe the museum-school relationship shows considerable potential for the future, particularly in light of the recent calls for strengthening the quality of instruction in science, the arts and the humanities in the schools. There would be no productive museum-school partnerships were it not for the capacity of museum professionals and educators to communicate on the local level about the assets of museums, the needs of schools and the ways in which the two can work together to design effective curriculums, making full use of unique local resources. But this kind of dialogue, however productive for the individual museum, has limited results—a better single program, a stronger relationship between one museum and the local school system. Conversations about mutual objectives need to take place at the level at which policy is made, among national and state leaders in education and museums. Only when the discussion about museums and schools is elevated to this level will it be taken as seriously as it should be.

As part of this policy discussion, we urge that special attention be given to nurturing the elements of a successful museum-school relationship at the most basic possible level: as an integral part of the undergraduate, graduate and continuing education of teachers. Learning based on objects is such a critical part of the educational process that no teacher should be permitted to overlook its potential.

There are models for this kind of effort. At the Philadelphia Museum of Art, Ted Katz designed a summer institute that introduced teachers to the museum as a learning resource and enhanced their ability to plan museum-related experiences for their students. Although the institute did not give teachers specific programs to take back to their schools, all the participants included mu-

seum experiences in their curriculum planning for the following year. The J. Paul Getty Trust's Institute for Educators on the Visual Arts is a similar effort dedicated to training teachers to assure that a quality education in the arts is available to children and adults. In Massachusetts, workshops sponsored by the Council on the Arts and Humanities and the state Department of Education help teachers "take the art experience one step further than the field trip." And at the Franklin Institute Science Museum in Philadelphia, the Atlantic Richfield Foundation supports a program to help local teachers learn how to use the museum's experiential education techniques in classroom science instruction.

◆ RECOMMENDATION 7: We recommend that the AAM and other professional education and museum organizations convene a national colloquium to begin an effective dialogue about the mutually enriching relationship museums and schools should have. We urge that the new consideration of the museum-school partnership involve leaders at all levels, with participation from government, business, the academic community, education and museums. This colloquium should consider the value of collaboration between museums and schools, the issues that need fresh approaches for the future and the practical means by which mutual goals can be realized at the state and local levels.

Museums and Independent Learning

Outside formal educational systems, a web of other opportunities for learning has developed, as education is recognized as a lifelong process that need not take place entirely within the confines of a formal structure or in pursuit of an academic degree. With the maturing of the baby boom generation and the accelerating rate of social change, the audience for learning in alternative environments will continue to swell. There will be more adults with more formal education and a more firmly instilled desire to continue their intellectual growth.

As increasing numbers of adults look for serious, legitimate opportunities to enrich their experiences and broaden their horizons, they will turn to museums, and rightly so. Museums are especially well suited to the kind of educational

Museums on Television

Many museum professionals are not yet convinced that museums and television make a good couple. The controversy often centers around the meaningful, firsthand experience museums provide and the belief that the attenuated nature of television viewing is the antithesis of that experience. Many museums, however, have proved that television programming and museums can be complementary.

Museums have been on television since the introduction of the technology. In 1949, for instance, the Los Angeles County Museum of Art won an award from the Southern California Association for Better Radio and Television for the best educational program in the area. In 1950 the Joslyn Art Museum in Omaha offered a biweekly series of television programs about the museum's collections and activities. The Montclair Art Museum in Montclair, New Jersey, featured a weaving demonstration in another broadcast. Since then, former St. Louis Zoo director Marlin Perkins has made "Wild Kingdom" a permanent fixture on public television. The Metropolitan Museum of Art's Department of Film and Television produces TV programs about many of the museum's permanent and special exhibitions, and the Smithsonian Institution recently joined the proponents of television with "Smithsonian World," one of the most elaborate museum-based series ever to air.

The aim of television programs for museums is often twofold. One goal is to entice more people to visit the museum for a firsthand experience. In Texas, the Corpus Christi Museum's weekly "Museum Open House" ran on local television for 20 years. The museum's director, Aalbert Heine, used specimens from the collection to stimulate discussion with 8 to 12 year olds. Publicity from the program, as well as its popular and charismatic host, have worked to the museum's advantage by increasing public participation.

A second goal is to stimulate interest in the subject matter by emphasizing the circumstances surrounding an object or an exhibition. David H. Katzive, president of Museum Television Production Services, says a critical decision for museums is the message they want to convey. He notes, for example, that the National Gallery of Art's award-winning film about Picasso's "Saltimbanques" is enriched by its incorporation of Parisian street scenes and images from a real circus, and the Metropolitan's "La Belle Epoque" is successful not only for the works of art or costumes that are shown, but because it skillfully recreates a historic period and captures the colorful personalities who were part of it.

The fear that television will deflect interest from the museum itself seems unfounded. And the experience of the publishing industry offers some reassurance, for popular series like "Brideshead Revisited" and "Buddenbrooks" actually create best sellers. With the increasing availability of cable TV and greater sophistication in museums' use of the medium, television may actually stimulate new interest in museums and enhance their communication with their audiences.

A Lifetime of Learning

The educational function of museums is a distinctly American contribution, and in the last two decades the expansion of education programs in this country has been impressive. In *Museums USA*, 67 percent of museums report that their educational efforts are increasing and will continue to grow. Hundreds of excellent programs are described in recent volumes that catalog activities related to art, the humanities and science and technology. Ethnic festivals and community events abound as museums make a special effort to reach out to blacks, hispanics, senior citizens, other minority groups and the economically disadvantaged.

In Michigan a program for senior citizens is stimulating an interest in family and personal history and fostering an appreciation for history in general. History Sharing Through Our Photographs (HISTOP) focuses on objects and nearly always includes a visit to a local museum. It was developed by Nancy Rosen with a small grant from the Michigan Council for the Humanities. The fundamental procedure is deceptively simple: a senior citizen chooses a few family photographs, brings them to the host museum or school and shows them to the students; then they just sit together and talk about them.

When the adults and children meet, conversation comes easily: "This picture was taken only a few miles from here in a logging camp in approximately 1888." One woman told of driving a wagon across Wyoming in her youth, intending to marry a cowboy. Many begin, "Here's another thing you probably never heard of. . . ." The pictures and the stories that go with them fascinate the children, and they soon began asking questions and adding stories of their own. In the words of one child, age 10, "The senior citizens told us more than we ever knew about history."

Building on HISTOP's success, a how-to-do-it guide and a traveling exhibit now take the show on the road. It has been repeated in cities and locations of all kinds—museums, libraries and community centers, at Girl Scout meetings and in elementary school classrooms. And it's just one example of how museum programs can engage the interests of new and varied audiences.

experience adults are seeking, both individually and with their families. Adults respond best to what educator Malcolm Knowles calls "androgogy"—the art and science of helping people learn for themselves. At the opposite end of the spectrum from the pedagogical model, which is most suited to teaching particular skills, androgogy describes one aspect of the learning that takes place in museums.

Adults constitute a large part of the group described in museum circles as "casual visitors." They visit museums less frequently in organized groups than do young people; they are more often alone or with friends or their families. The motivation for their visit varies according to the set of experiences they bring with them and the nature of the occasion—whether they come as an individual, a parent, a friend.

Adults can be spontaneous, resourceful learners. Their relationship to what they are learning is often intensely personal and should not be distanced by didactic methods unsuited to the adult inclination and the adult mind. If museums are to have a lasting educational impact on adult visitors, they must appeal to their special needs.

The voluntary nature of the learning experience in museums can be compatible with the interests of all casual visitors, but it is particularly appropriate for adults. For several years, museum educators and administrators have been devoting considerable attention to adults in anticipation of what they know will be a greater demand for programs and activities geared to the adult learner. Some examples:

▪ A *New York Times* article described the Smithsonian Institution's Resident Associate Program as "the largest and most successful culture college in the country." The student body is huge—nearly 200,000 adults and still growing—and the curriculum includes as many as 900 offerings each year. Through this program, adults have participated in symposiums on topics from politics to film, walking tours of Washington neighborhoods and excursions to New York City museums, workshops on computers and courses in visual appreciation.

▪ The substantive training many museums provide their volunteers is an attraction of volunteer work in museums as well as a form of continuing education. At the Field Museum of Natural History in Chicago, for example, an intensive 13-week program includes an introduction to four scientific disciplines, training in the presentation of natural history and instruction in using objects with a variety of audiences.

▪ Many adults look to museums as a place for family outings, and some museums have expanded their program offerings in response. At Washington's Capital Children's Museum, computer courses teach adults and children together. The Boston Children's Museum has extensive family programs, including a discovery kit that can be rented and taken home. At Old Sturbridge Village in Massachusetts, there is a special winter workshop in which families are transported back to the 19th century through role-playing techniques.

◆ RECOMMENDATION 8: We urge that museums continue to build on their success as centers of learning by providing high-quality educational experiences for people of all ages, but, in recognition of the increasing median age of our population, that they pay new attention to their programs for adults. Museum professionals must consider ways to introduce their institutions to the adult public as sources of intellectual enrichment, as places where learning can be spontaneous and personal and as opportunities for growth and thinking as well as seeing.

4 Guiding the Values of Museums

A leader's role," former New Jersey Bell president Chester Barnard has said, "is to harness the social forces in an organization, to shape and guide values." How fitting this is for museums, where excellence is often the fruit of great leadership. Forceful leaders define, defend and challenge what museums stand for. Whether they are acting in behalf of particular institutions or the community of museums, they are the link between purpose and practice. Effective leadership makes a museum—or museums in general—a visible, energetic part of society, with a demonstrated service quite different from, but comparable in importance to, the services other institutions provide. Leaders establish an atmosphere conducive to creativity and excellence, while keeping a firm focus on the museum's purpose and potential. Only with good leadership can growth be meaningful and change productive. Leadership is, in short, the key to implementing much of what this commission recommends as an agenda for the future of American museums.

These are times that require sound and innovative leadership by museum staffs, directors and trustees. The first chapter of this report described the integral connection of museums to the rest of American life and the societal trends that are having profound effects on museums today. The strain on economic resources in museums, the plethora of legal issues ranging from conflict of interest to illicit traffic in art objects, the tangle of federal and state regulations, the move toward collaboration with other institutions—all these are testing the foresight and flexibility of museum leaders.

The professional standards movement of the past 15 years has focused deliberately on the mission of museums as institutions—their distinctive service to society. Up to this point in our report,

we, too, have talked primarily about institutional mission and our belief that it must be impressed more vividly on the public consciousness. As we consider new questions of leadership and professionalism for the future, however, we would like to add another dimension to the discussion. The functions of museums as *institutions* are clearly defined, if not yet as widely understood as we in museums would like them to be. But there is no common agreement on the form of museums as *organizations*—the characteristics that make their institutional mission viable. Like any enterprise with a particular mission, the museum has special organizational qualities that ultimately determine the style of leadership it needs and the definition of "professionalism" in its operational mode. The museum as an *organization* is the mechanism used to carry out the mission of the museum as an *institution*. The organization provides the environment that can make possible both innovation and the articulation of the museum's traditional values. Clarity of purpose in the organization is as important as clarity of mission in the institution.

Review of the functions of museums as institutions and analysis, in that light, of their characteristics as organizations are the first steps in assuring that their internal structures will continue to be effective in our changing society.

The Museum as Institution

The mission of museums as institutions grows out of tradition and is shaped by public need. It is to collect and preserve the evidence of the natural and physical world and of human accomplish-

Specialized Museum Associations

Through its network of professional organizations, the museum community ensures the representation of both shared and special interests. New and vibrant members of this network are groups that serve museums preserving and celebrating minority cultures, like the African-American Museums Association.

The intellectual ferment of the 1960s that gave rise to the discipline of African-American studies had another by-product—the growth and expansion of black museums. There are now more than 100 museums dedicated to collecting objects representing African and African-American culture. Intellectually diverse and widely varying in their approach to education, African-American museums do have a common goal—to demonstrate through their collections and programs the African influences in American life and culture. They also strive to explain relationships among cultures and to educate their constituencies, especially the black community, about the importance of collecting and documenting objects relating to black American history.

Since 1978 the AAMA has been instrumental in bringing these institutions together and promoting the philosophy that a committed national network of African-American museums will strengthen museums at the local level. As the single representative and principal voice of the African-American museum community, the AAMA is especially interested in helping museums refine their education programs so that the richness of the African-American experience can be better understood and appreciated.

The AAMA, which is based in Washington, D.C., works to meet needs not addressed by the older museum service organizations. It keeps abreast of developments in the profession at large and gives its 106 members a means of initiating common action. A primary emphasis is professional training for staff in African-American museums. The association organizes annual meetings, publishes a quarterly newsletter, sponsors regional workshops on collections planning and interpretation and supports a formal internship program to encourage minority students to enter the museum profession. Plans include a two-year series of management workshops and a systematic survey of black museums in order to document their condition, aspirations and requirements.

Like dozens of other museum service organizations, the African-American Museums Association represents and serves a particular segment of the museum community. Together these professional organizations are a large, active network that helps ensure the quality of museums as a whole.

ment, and to use those collections and related ideas to contribute to human knowledge and understanding.

This mission has been the focal point of the effort by museum professionals to articulate and implement standards and ethical principles for their institutions and their work. The logical first step in this process was the development of a definition of a museum that could be accepted by the profession at large. The American Association of Museums' Accreditation Program has accomplished this task. It defines a museum as "an organized and permanent nonprofit institution, essentially educational or esthetic in purpose, with professional staff, which owns and utilizes tangible objects, cares for them and exhibits them to the public on some regular schedule." With this definition as a starting point, the profession has developed standards for judging an institution's effectiveness at fulfilling its own individual purpose.

The Accreditation Program is the cornerstone of these measures of quality. To date, 579 museums of all sizes and disciplines have been accredited in this program of self-evaluation and peer review. In 1978 the profession adopted *Museum Ethics* as the broad statement by which individual museums can shape and test their principles and policies. Guidelines for trustees have been developed, too, and codes of ethics for specialists such as conservators, curators, public relations officers, security personnel and registrars have been adopted or are being drawn up. Professional standards have been adopted for museum stores and proposed for museum training programs and internships. In addition, the certification of museum professionals and training programs is currently under active discussion.

The movement to define standards of quality in museums and museum work has paralleled the growing need for public institutions of all kinds to be accountable for their actions, but it is also a natural step in the evolution of a profession. A natural step in the evolution of a museum is the achievement of accredited status, and it is the view of this commission that every museum should aspire to that end. Uniformity among museums is not the objective; every museum that undergoes the accreditation process is considered in light of its own stated purpose and the resources at its command. But the aspiration to achieve accreditation indicates that the institution is devoted to excellence and guided by sound

Museum Accreditation

Concern for quality has always been a hallmark of museums—in the acquisition of collections, their display in exhibition galleries, the technical processes that must take place behind the scenes. Museums have always been concerned, too, with self-evaluation and self-improvement in the achievement of quality. Professional organizations have actively worked to help museums achieve the very best. Publications such as the American Association of Museums' *Museum Accounting Handbook, Museum Registration Methods* and *Museum Trusteeship* are the standard technical guides for the field. The association's Museum Assessment Program, funded by the Institute of Museum Services, provides a structured consultancy designed especially to help improve the programs and operations of small museums. Since its inception in 1981, more than 900 museums have benefited.

But the program that has done more than any other to raise standards throughout the museum field is the Accreditation Program developed by the AAM in 1970. Established by the profession for the profession, it employs self-evaluation and peer review to assure the quality of America's museums and the quality of the experience of those who use them—from the casual visitor to the serious scholar. The program is also designed to enhance the performance and perception of museums and to encourage them to engage in continuing self-assessment.

In its 14 years of operation the Accreditation Program has accredited 579 museums. The maintenance of standards is as important as achieving them, and 159 museums have been reaccredited in a mandatory procedure initiated every five to 10 years. The American Association of Zoological Parks and Aquariums also has an official accreditation program. It has accredited 72 zoos and aquariums and has mandated that its total institutional membership of 187 be accredited by December 31, 1985. Some zoos and aquariums have been accredited by the AAM's program as well.

Museums that have gone through the accreditation process report a great many benefits. "We got a little decal and a plaque suitable for framing," says Carl Hansen, director of the Frankenmuth Historical Museum in Michigan. "But," he continues, "what we really got out of it was a 27-page operational manual governing the collection and the administration of the museum, a new fire and security system, redesigned permanent exhibit areas and defined roles of staff and board committee structure. We gained a new awareness and interest in our image in terms of programs, publications, fund-raising efforts, training of staff and publicity. The museum staff and board saw that accreditation was a critical turning point for the organization; we were committed to the professional standards of the field." Other museums report that the accreditation process and its mandatory self-assessment led to the development of sound written policies, better relations between staff and governing board, improvements in the physical plant, strengthened credibility in the community and more successful fund-raising efforts.

Museums of all types, sizes, disciplines, ages and budgets are eligible for accreditation, and the AAM Accreditation Commission has, over the years, expanded its guidelines to make the program applicable to a variety of museums, including planetariums, botanical gardens and arboretums, science-technology centers, art centers and historic sites. To be considered, a museum must first of all fulfill every aspect of the basic definition of a museum, which was developed for the program with great care. For the purposes of accreditation a museum is "an organized and permanent nonprofit institution, essentially educational or esthetic in purpose, with professional staff, which owns and utilizes tangible objects, cares for them and exhibits them to the public on some regular schedule."

Not all America's nearly 5,000 museums meet these requirements, but Lawrence Reger, director of the AAM, estimates that, in addition to those already accredited, approximately 500 museums are at the right point in their development to apply. Helping other museums to achieve the standards of accreditation will be a principal effort of the AAM in the coming years. The association's Museum Assessment Program is a key element in that effort.

As standards throughout the field are raised, so, too, are the requirements for accreditation. The Accreditation Program will continue to set the highest goals of achievement for the profession and be a catalyst for the development of America's museums. As Reger insists, "We can do no more than work toward these high standards. . . . We must do no less."

leadership. And the accreditation of individual museums promotes high standards and institutional self-confidence throughout the museum community.

As they have defined their mission clearly through the professional standards movement, museums and the museum profession have come of age. They both depend for their healthy future development on their leaders' ability to know, and continually refine, the ethical and professional basis of their actions. Maintaining standards is a continuing process, the obligation a mature profession has to itself as well as to its broader public.

The Museum as Organization

We suggest that there are three organizational characteristics that relate both to the museum's status as a nonprofit institution and to its individual mission:

- The goal of the museum as organization is to carry out the accepted mission of museums in a manner appropriate to the particular institution. Each museum gives those activities its own special character.

- The organization is driven to excel at its goals by such factors as institutional pride, the incentive to meet professional standards and the desire to maintain a tradition of excellence and service.

- The success of the organization is measured by its ability to meet high professional standards, define its constituencies responsibly, communicate its goals to those constituencies and involve them in the full complexity of its mission. The organization is the mechanism by which the purpose of the institution is achieved.

Two current ideas about the leadership and management of nonprofit institutions are affecting museum organization. The first is the attempt to measure a museum's success solely by its balance sheet, and the second is the move toward choosing men and women from outside the profession to head museums. Since these ideas, while well-intentioned, are not consistent with the values of museums, we believe they indicate the need for a firmer grasp of the museum as organization.

In response to current political and economic trends, there has been discussion about the potential for financial self-sufficiency in nonprofit institutions. Income-producing enterprises can be beneficial, and many museums have wisely developed strategies for increasing earned income. Fiscal competence, aggressive pursuit of adequate resources and wise allocation of those resources should characterize every museum. But the assumption that a balanced budget or a net surplus is the only measure of a museum's quality, or that profit is the measure of a program's success, obscures the important differences between profit and nonprofit organizations and blurs the distinction between good leadership and good management. As public relations executive William Ruder reminded a group of museum trustees, "Our function is not to be like a corporation that worships at the altar of 15 percent compounded growth. Our business is to help people enrich their lives."

If the costs of providing a public service were fully passed along to the consumer, a nonprofit organization's service function would be obviated. In the case of museums, the cost of the stewardship of irreplaceable resources cannot be measured; nor can the resources themselves be assigned a price. The notion of service is an unalterable operating principle for museums, and for other nonprofit organizations as well. As Thomas M. Messer, director of the Solomon R. Guggenheim Museum, has pointed out:

> Institutions like museums, universities and libraries have a different role to play in society, a non-economic role. If fund raising priorities in any of the spiritual realms take precedence over their raison d'être, the long-range result may be a flattening of that purpose.

The second indicator that the museum as organization needs clarification is the view that museums are better headed by people outside the profession than by those trained and experienced in the scholarly and educational pursuits of the institution. In some museums the top position is shared. When the trustees of the Metropolitan Museum of Art decided in 1977 to appoint both a paid president and a director, the former to serve as administrative head of the museum and the latter responsible for its scholarly and educational functions, many large museums followed suit.

While these models may have advantages, the underlying assumption is that men and women trained and experienced in the museum profession do not have the managerial skills to be effective chief executive officers. This contrived dichotomy causes an organization to miss the opportunity professionals can offer it. The motivation to be a good manager is stronger when personal, professional and institutional values correspond.

Today's museum director has a formidable array of responsibilities, but the trends toward separating administrative functions and programmatic functions and toward looking outside the profession for leadership can be a misapplication of the business perspective. There is no question that techniques adopted from business can put a museum in a strong organizational position to strive for excellence and accommodate change. But these techniques cannot alone make a museum fulfill its mission successfully. The pragmatic decisions must be made in direct relation to esthetic, educational and scientific ends. An effective museum leader—whether scholar or M.B.A. or both—must first understand, believe in and speak for the values of the institution.

Fortunately, there is a growing body of knowledge about nonprofit leadership and management that is encouraging the museum profession to examine the organizational qualities of museums. Recognition of the unique nature of nonprofit institutions moves them out of the for-profit realm of management theory, where they have never been comfortably situated. Nonprofit management is now part of the curriculum in major business schools such as Yale, Wharton, Northwestern and Harvard. Organizations doing commendable research into the philosophy, structure and management of nonprofit institutions include Independent Sector, Yale's Institution for Social and Policy Studies and the Association of Governing Boards of Universities and Colleges.

Museum management, too, is more commonly studied today. This trend is moving the museum profession toward greater sophistication in museum leadership, management and organization. The agendas of professional meetings are filled with panel discussions and speeches about planning, financial management and personnel procedures; workshops and seminars sponsored by professional organizations frequently deal with management issues. Management courses offered by Museums Collaborative, Inc., and the J. Paul

Getty Trust with the Art Museum Association of America and the University of California, Berkeley, are aimed at professionals in midcareer.

Now the museum community must set its own organizational standards, just as it set its own institutional standards. The profession must define and strengthen the unique organizational qualities of museums and the accompanying measures of good leadership and institutional success. One cannot judge the success of a museum in quite the same way as the success of a business or, for that matter, the success of another nonprofit institution. There are indeed tangible measures, but the intangible ones—the quality of a museum's fundamental pursuits—are at once more important and more difficult to grasp.

As a beginning, we suggest four areas that should be examined closely with a view toward describing the form of museums as organizations: the operation of the museum governance system; the professional working climate in museums, including attention to the motivations and incentives for museum work; excellence in small museums; and the need for information that describes the American museum universe.

Governance: A Working Partnership

The governance system of American museums has long been the focus of spirited debate. Our museums are governed by boards of trustees— "private individuals who, as a body, hold their institution's assets in trust as fiduciaries for the public," as the standard handbook, *Museum Trusteeship*, puts it. Unlike trustees in the rest of the world's museums, trustees in our museums are volunteers. This tradition gives American museums their independent and democratic character, but it also breeds misunderstanding of purpose and a confusion about the delegation of responsibilities between board and staff. The difference between trustees and staff, on paper, sounds straightforward. According to *Museum Trusteeship*, "museum trustees make policy . . . and monitor the execution of that policy." Although they are ultimately responsible for the success of the museum, they "must remain aloof from the actual execution" of its day-to-day operations. The theory is that in this way they can retain the objectivity required for leadership.

The application, or misapplication, of this principle is a central issue facing the museum governance system. The clear-cut assignment of policy

making to trustees and policy implementation to staff is sometimes too simplistic to be practical. The ground rules are particularly unclear about what constitutes "policy" and how narrow or broad policy-making authority should be.

In addition, the obligations inherent in trusteeship are increasingly complex, as museums must meet growing numbers of fiscal, legal and societal requirements. Old roles are changing; just as the job of museum director is no longer genteel employment, so the position of trustee is no longer just a source of social cachet. Today's trustee must be knowledgeable about the functions of the museum, in tune with the needs and interests of its constituencies, committed to ensuring the museum's financial stability. Most trustees are leaders in their own professions and communities and accustomed to playing leading roles, but many have a limited range of experience in matters relating to museums. They are not always in a strong position to make appropriate judgments about the policies and programs of the museum.

Although today's museum trustees are clearly interested in giving expertise as well as money, a recent study by Israel Unterman and Richard Hart Davis of more than 100 nonprofit boards revealed that "business executives who become trustees too often fail to apply their managerial expertise to their volunteer efforts . . . a void that is most apparent in the formulation and implementation of strategy." Trustees may not be effectively stimulated to contribute, either. Edward M. Warburg told participants at a recent symposium on "Who Controls Museums?" that being a trustee is "a form of Seconal, efficient but non-involving." If that is the case, the system of museum governance is not working well.

The Unterman and Davis study attributed part of the nonprofit governance problem to board structures. Museums, like other nonprofit organizations, typically have boards of 30 or more members; corporate boards, on the other hand, are usually limited to 10 or 15. Boards of museums in the commission's monitoring system ranged in size from nine to 50. Similarly, committee structures and responsibilities vary tremendously from board to board, as do selection procedures, length of service and the thoroughness of orientation programs introducing new trustees to the museum's purpose and operations. Regular self-evaluation, with special attention to the effectiveness of policy planning, is not generally a part of museum board operations.

But the weaknesses of museum governance cannot all be laid at the doorstep of trustees or the trustee system. The role of staff members is equally demanding and complex. The museum director must be effective at guiding the institution toward achieving professional standards, skilled at management and fund raising, forceful in asserting a presence for the museum in the community and informed about the intellectual significance of the museum's collections. Directors want to be perceived as the leaders of their institutions; some feel that as trained and experienced professionals they know best how to proceed in matters of museum policy and practice, so they chafe at the participation of nonprofessionals. The governance of publicly funded museums often is further complicated by the fact that their directors commonly report both to a politically appointed board of trustees and a body of elected officials, and not infrequently to a board of a private "friends" group as well.

We recognize the wisdom of lay governance of our institutions, as it ensures objective policy making. We do not question the governance system itself, but how to make it work better for museums now and in the future. We call for a partnership of trustees and staff that can offer strong, cooperative and forward-thinking leadership. They are working in the same institutions and toward the same mission. Both staff and trustees must have a real part in formulating and promoting this mission; they should not simply confront each other over the way to achieve it.

There is a good framework within which effective trusteeship can be encouraged. On a national level, the AAM's Trustee Committee encourages trustee participation in the broader museum profession and promotes the importance of responsible, informed trusteeship. Museum trustees meet regularly on the regional, state and local levels. The Texas Association of Museums, for example, sponsors an annual meeting for trustees; the New England Museums Association and the Southeastern Museums Conference have special programs for trustees at their annual meetings. Publications, workshops and seminars are valuable resources. In professional organizations such as the Association of Art Museum Directors and the Association of Science Museum Directors, there is also a good framework for encouraging leadership among directors.

Trustee education must become a high priority. It is the director's responsibility to design pro-

Museum Volunteers

According to a recent Gallup survey, 31 percent of American adults volunteer on a regular basis, serving, on the average, two hours per week; 10 percent serve seven hours or more. Some of this volunteer assistance is in the field of education, including museums. Jane Konrad, president of the United States Association of Museum Volunteers, says that more than 70,000 volunteers serve in the nation's museums, and the number grows steadily every year. The museums in the commission's monitoring system report volunteer groups ranging in size from 12 to 300. At the Smithsonian Institution alone, more than 4,000 volunteers give more than 450,000 hours of service annually. History museums in the Northeast Museums Conference have two or three volunteers for every paid staff member.

Museum volunteers do work of all kinds. In 1983, volunteers at the Milwaukee Public Museum donated 32,000 hours, working under the supervision of staff in projects involving research, cataloging and the restoration and maintenance of collections. Docents gave tours to adults, children and the handicapped. Volunteers served in the museum shop, library, photography section and publications department. A volunteer garden club shares a greenhouse with members of the museum's botany section. There is virtually no aspect of museum operations unassisted by volunteers.

Elsewhere, museum volunteers perform a different array of services. At the Museum of Science in Boston, Project Eye-Opener recruits teenagers to help inner-city children enjoy the museum. Mystic Seaport in Connecticut has a 25-member Gung-Ho Squad that helps paid staff maintain the historic vessels.

Volunteerism used to be the undisputed province of the nonworking woman, but that image is changing. There are now more volunteers who hold full-time jobs. A recent survey in New York City, for example, reports that more than 70 percent of the men and women seeking volunteer jobs are working people. Retirees are also joining the volunteer ranks in large numbers, and many bring specialized and valuable expertise to the museum. Corporations often encourage their employees to get involved in community activities, and a few have experimented with allowing employees to do community-service volunteer work on company time.

Just as the profile of volunteers is changing, so is volunteer style and purpose. Museum volunteers now expect greater responsibility and opportunity for personal growth, and museums are requiring more rigorous training programs. The Smithsonian's Hirshhorn Museum and Sculpture Garden, for example, requires its docents to enroll in university art history courses. The Baldwin Heritage Museum Association in Elberta, Alabama, arranged an eight-week course for volunteers that included the history and philosophy of museums and collections care and management.

Museums are asking more of their volunteers. And they're getting what they ask for in a new breed of committed, versatile people who perform integral services in all kinds of museums.

grams to enlighten trustees about the mission, standards and practices of the museum and their responsibilities as board members. Directors must make time to discuss important museum issues with trustees. Good orientation and continuing education make for effective trusteeship and a sound trustee-staff partnership that promotes the best interests of the museum.

We believe it is time to take a close look at the system of museum governance, identify models that work well and determine how trustees and museum professionals together can make it provide more effective leadership for museums in the future.

◆ RECOMMENDATION 9: Effective leadership for museums emerges from the ability of trustees to shape and guide the missions of their institutions. In the interest of making governance work better, we ask that a special, independent task force of trustees, directors and leaders of other nonprofit institutions with similar governance structures be convened at the initiative of the American Association of Museums. It should assess the quality of governance of American museums, examining such matters as the board-staff relationship and the selection and composition of boards. It should also identify the kinds of assistance that would equip both trustees and staff to provide the leadership museums will need in the future.

Can Museum Work Be Its Own Reward?

Together with its collections, a museum's staff is its most valuable resource. The work of staff members gives the museum its character and individuality; they communicate the museum's mission to the public, and, through the programs and exhibitions they develop, they give the collections life.

Incentives for museum work are traditionally related to the service mission of museums, with the rewards often taking the form of personal satisfaction, a sense of accomplishment or the opportunity to work in an atmosphere of creativity and intellectual independence. Perhaps unwittingly, the U.S. Department of Labor exemplified the sense that museum work is its own reward in the title of the pamphlet, *Career Opportunities in Art Museums, Zoos and Other Interesting Places.*

In a report prepared for Yale's Institution for Social and Policy Studies, social scientist Dennis Young says professionals who choose careers in nonprofit organizations create their own motivation for employment. They are inspired by professional interest or by the character of the milieu in which they work, and they often accept lower salaries than they could command elsewhere. Yet personnel management often fails to meet the commitment of its staff, as managers seem unwilling or unable to channel the motivation of employees by devising suitable rewards for their personal commitment to quality.

A museum professional's tangible rewards, like the rewards in most other nonprofit organizations, are limited. Salaries and benefits lag behind those in professions that require comparable levels of education and experience. Dennis Young points to two factors as possible explanations:

> certain benefits of the pleasant work environment, including access to educational materials and programs and the professional atmosphere, and . . . the frugal attitude of some trustees who, for various reasons, may expect a high degree of selflessness and dedication from employees.

A dramatic example of the inequity of museum salaries in relation to responsibilities can be seen in a classified advertisement that recently appeared in *Aviso*, the newsletter of the American Association of Museums:

> Curator of Collections. Person to supervise the largest collection of ————. Responsibilities include assisting in the development of a long-range plan for collections management, preparation and implementation of a conservation plan, directing research and assisting with exhibition planning, serving in administrative and budgetary capacities. Qualifications: academic training in ———— and three years' museum experience in a curatorial department. Writing ability important for publications and for preparation of funding packages. Salary: $13,000–$14,000.

Comparative salary statistics can be a useful management tool, but attempts to tabulate salary data for museums have been sporadic, usually regional and limited in scope. None, for instance, provide information about experience or training—two factors that affect the determination of salary. This lack of data must be corrected.

Although we are mindful of the intangible benefits of a museum career, we are concerned that salaries for museum work are not competitive with those for similar fields, even in the nonprofit sector. The situation is particularly critical in light of the extensive training and varied experience required of today's museum professionals and the need to retain them and to encourage talented future leaders. The caliber of museum leadership and the quality of museums are in jeopardy.

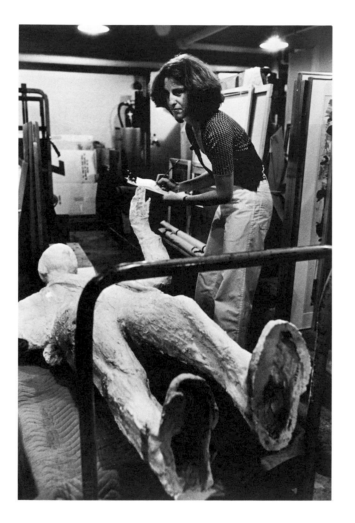

◆ RECOMMENDATION 10: Museum work merits professional compensation. If the salaries for professional staff in museums do not increase, the museum profession and museums nationwide will suffer the loss of talented people qualified to perform demanding and complex functions. We urge that each museum develop responsible compensation policies and practices that bring its salaries and benefits into line with professional work for which similar education and experience are required.

To describe the museum work force more completely, the museum community needs a professional personnel study that presents salary information and describes working conditions in the context of geographic location, training, experience, and level and nature of responsibility. This information is essential to a better understanding of the caliber of professional needed to run this country's museums. This study should be initiated by the American Association of Museums working in cooperation with other museum service organizations.

Opportunity in the Museum Work Force

We are also concerned about the status of minorities and women in the museum work force. The cultural pluralism that museums celebrate is not manifested in the composition of museum staffs. It is a troublesome truth, not an unfair stereotype, that the museum work force is largely white and dominated in the upper echelons by men. Although there are virtually no quantitative data about the work force in museums, it would be hard to dispute the fact that few minorities hold professional positions in museums and few women can be found in high levels of management. Anyone who has attended a professional museum meeting can attest to the absence of minorities among delegates. The museums in our monitoring system reported that only 5 percent of their staffs are black, and most of those people work in maintenance and security jobs. Though many women work in museums, they do not generally hold jobs at high administrative levels. There are few women directors of major museums. The Association of Art Museum Directors, which represents 130 museums, has only seven women members. The Association of Science Museum Directors, which represents 65 natural science museums, has only three. Certain functions—jobs in museum education, for example, or working with children—have been stereotyped as "women's work." Salary inequities are also telling. There are no data for minority salaries, but an Association of Science-Technology Centers survey shows that in all but two of 18 categories—registrar and exhibits technician—women were paid less than men for comparable work.

Redressing the inequities of minority representation in the museum work force cannot be accomplished simply by calling for equal opportunity or affirmative action. So few blacks, Asians, hispanics, native Americans or other minorities work in professional positions in museums—with the exception of minority museums—that the perception of opportunity simply does not exist. The problem is compounded by the fact that relatively few minority young people enter the academic fields that traditionally produce museum professionals. As long as these conditions persist, the potential for change in the racial and ethnic composition of museum staffs will be limited. Therefore museums must seek to change the conditions by exploring ways of interesting minority young people in museum work.

The solutions for women involve breaking down long-held attitudes. This will, of course, be difficult. Our society is not yet used to seeing women in leadership roles. In museums, the barriers are compounded by the tradition that the director's role calls for a married man, with his wife as social partner.

In higher education a concerted effort has moved women onto upward career paths. Eight years ago the American Council on Education (ACE) started a special program to bring qualified women into position for career advancement by introducing them to administrators with responsibility for hiring. Two hundred sixty colleges and

The Smithsonian's Career Awareness Program

The choices many minority young people make while in their early teens limit their future career opportunities. If they do not understand what knowledge and skills are required for certain kinds of work, they may not enroll in the high school classes they need to prepare them for college. These choices then keep them out of contention for advancement in many professions.

In the belief that this may be one reason few minorities work in museums, in 1982 the Office of Elementary and Secondary Education at the Smithsonian Institution began to introduce minority young people to career opportunities in museums through the Career Awareness Program (CAP). Ninth-graders from throughout the Washington, D.C., area were invited to school assemblies to hear about careers at the Smithsonian. Then those who wanted to learn more met with the museum's conservators, exhibit designers, writers, educators and curators and participated in workshops on individual careers. Each student then had a one-day "externship" with a museum professional.

Since CAP's beginning, several hundred minority students have been introduced each year to careers in the various Smithsonian museums. Of those, more than 100 have participated in the full program. And program planners are pleased with the results. As the CAP advisory committee hoped, the students showed an increased knowledge of career opportunities in museums. Some said they would like to be museum volunteers; others found role models in the professionals they had met. They also reported learning about new things in new ways. As one girl described it, the museum is "better than school and books."

For most of the students, CAP was their first museum experience; for all, it was the first time they had been "behind the scenes." Said one, "For me, the special part of the program was just getting to be inside the Air and Space Museum. I remember driving with my dad once and we passed that place. And I remember thinking to myself how much I would like to go inside there and see what it really looked like. Well, now I've been there, and it's as good as I thought it was going to be."

The Smithsonian is offering graduates of the program opportunities for continued involvement with the institution. CAP students are regularly invited to attend lectures and seminars, and during the summer of 1984, 16 of them had jobs at the Smithsonian as part of Washington's Summer Youth Employment Program.

CAP is helping to build a pool of qualified minorities for museum work and continues to introduce new audiences to museums. In February 1983, shortly after CAP began, the Smithsonian established a special committee to investigate why so few blacks, Asians and hispanics visited its museums. Said Edward R. Rivinus, committee cochairman, "It is evident that the Smithsonian appeals to the traditional audience—WASP and educated. We want to find out what the problem is, and what we can do about it." As generations of CAP graduates continue to visit the museums and some return to work there, perhaps these questions won't need to be posed so keenly.

universities have women presidents today, an increase from 5 percent to 9 percent of the total; the ACE considers the new network program part of the reason. Such an approach could be adopted by the museum community.

The underrepresentation of minorities and women is a complex situation that will not change overnight, but it must change. In a society where occupational stereotypes are at last diminishing, museums must not lag behind. Of equal concern is the effect the composition of the museum work force has on the capacity of museums to show and interpret all facets of our heritage from a fair and balanced perspective.

◆RECOMMENDATION 11: We strongly believe the museum community must address the underrepresentation of minorities in the museum work force generally and the underrepresentation of women in the higher levels of management. It is the obligation of inherently pluralistic institutions such as museums to ensure that their organizational structures reflect cultural diversity and equal opportunity. The museum community should explore ways to interest minority young people in museum work at the high school level through special programs designed to direct them toward undergraduate and graduate academic disciplines that lead to museum careers. Boards of trustees and directors should give high priority to hiring qualified minorities and women in positions of leadership and authority and providing opportunities for them to advance up the career ladder.

Professional museum organizations can help both minorities and women by asserting that greater opportunity for these groups is a sign of high professional standards and by serving as networks of information and support.

Small Museums and Excellence

The concerns of small museums arose frequently during the course of this commission's work. These institutions are just as important to the community of museums as large institutions. No one museum can be all things to all people, and this is the reason smaller institutions are so essential a part of the museum domain. They often represent special interests—ethnic, cultural, regional—and they serve their audiences in ways larger museums cannot. They are links to particular eras of history, showcases for young artists, preservers of racial or ethnic heritage. In small communities, these museums are frequently centers of cultural life.

Small museums are to larger ones what the family business is to the large corporation: a microcosm of the organization, not a less-than-perfect imitation. We have heard about a number of important issues from our colleagues in small museums, and the AAM's Museum Assessment Program, a consulting service designed especially for small museums, has helped identify their most pressing needs. In requiring assistance in collections care, long-range planning, fund raising, educational programming and audience and membership development, and in often requiring clarification of the role and responsibilities of their boards of trustees, small museums are no different from large museums, and their interests are reflected throughout in this report. This holds true, too, for the issues of leadership and professionalism discussed in this chapter.

Size obviates neither quality nor the need for quality; the size of a budget, staff or building should not restrict the drive to excel. Good leadership is critical for all museums. It is the source of the motivation to achieve the best that resources will permit, the wisdom to know the limits of possibility for the institution and the sensitivity to the professional needs of both volunteer and salaried staff members. We recognize, however, that small and developing institutions sometimes need special professional assistance. It is this last point to which we want to address a recommendation.

We concur with the conviction of the Accreditation Commission of the American Association of Museums that paid professional staff ensure the continuity in policy and programming necessary to a museum operation of high quality. We recognize that developing museums must first generate sufficient community support before a staff's professional expertise could be used effectively. But we are convinced that to achieve excellence museums with all-volunteer staffs must include in their plans the goal of hiring trained, salaried, professional staff.

◆ RECOMMENDATION 12: In the firm belief that size is not a criterion for excellence, we encourage programs that provide information and training for professionals and volunteers in small and developing museums. The education of staff enables

The Regional Conference of Historical Agencies

Achieving high professional standards is a goal of many museums individually, but in New York State smaller historical societies and museums are meeting this challenge together. The Regional Conference of Historical Agencies (RCHA), in Manlius, New York, is a consortium of institutions with budgets averaging between $50,000 and $100,000 a year, but it includes a substantial number of museums and historical societies with budgets smaller than $1,000. Founded in 1971 and receiving substantial and reliable support from the New York Council on the Arts since then, the RCHA makes it a point to direct its services toward those museums that cannot pay for them and, in many cases, cannot benefit from any of the other established museum associations.

With a membership of 350 historical agencies, RCHA is able to offer many and varied services. Member institutions receive both technical and news-oriented publications. Hans J. Finke, program director of RCHA, oversees the consortium's workshop series—25 one-day programs on various topics—but he maintains that among the most important services the conference provides is the sale of acid-free and archival materials. RCHA purchases these materials at a bulk rate and sells them to member institutions at or just above cost. "For a small historical agency," Finke says, "the savings are very substantial, and the materials make a big difference in the quality of collections care and maintenance."

Recently RCHA received a grant from Apple Computer, Inc., to set up a computer network designed as an information service linking agencies across the state, including the Division of Historical and Anthropological Services. Finke says that efficiency in coordinating speakers and workshops and establishing an information service are priorities of the Apple grant. Using the computer to compile a statewide inventory of objects in historical society collections is far down the road but definitely a thought for the future.

Much like the Museum Assessment Program of the American Association of Museums, RCHA offers curatorial consulting services to its members. For little or no charge, RCHA staff members or outside consultants visit small historical agencies aspiring to achieve professional standards and help them address problems in both administration and interpretation. The program is specifically targeted toward museums with no funds for professional consultations or, in some cases, even for salaries.

Since RCHA provides an essential service to museums and historical societies that might otherwise be outside the usual professional networks, it is a great boon not only to its members but to the achievement of high standards in all corners of the museum domain.

The Louisiana Association of Museums

The South has a wealth of small history museums with local or regional collections. They have typically developed in isolation, and their collections, archival materials and interpretive programs are generally not known beyond their communities. But in Louisiana, that situation is changing.

The Louisiana Association of Museums (LAM), founded in 1979, has taken important steps to address the need for greater interaction and sharing of resources among these institutions. In January 1983, with a $10,000 grant from the Louisiana Committee for the Humanities and support from the Louisiana Division of the Arts and the Louisiana State Museum, LAM undertook a survey of the state's museums, university galleries, archival centers, libraries and other institutions that have spaces or resources for exhibitions and/or curatorial and educational responsibilities for cultural collections. The objective was to establish a centralized, cataloged information system to help institutions locate and use resources in the state's museums and to increase cooperative endeavors among them.

So far the project has resulted in the first directory of Louisiana museums and exhibition spaces. The profiles of each institution describe their mission, traveling exhibition preferences and availability of media and publication resources, as well as location, telephone number and hours open to the public. In June 1984 LAM sponsored three workshops around the state to introduce museum professionals and volunteers to the survey. Planning is now under way for a fourth statewide workshop on the LAM project.

Other plans include a promotional brochure and poster highlighting Louisiana museums that will be distributed by the state's Office of Tourism. Supplements to the directory on in-state traveling exhibitions, publications, media resources and collections will also be developed and distributed. With the cooperation of Louisiana State University, materials from the project will be put on the university's microcomputer so they can be regularly updated, supplemented and made available to LAM members and interested university scholars.

LAM's work has been called a "model project." The Southern Arts Federation is interested in replicating it on a regional basis, and a similar project at the national level is under discussion. Efforts like this cannot help but encourage small museums to make their assets known and appreciated by a wider public.

museums to fulfill their obligations to their collections and their public. We suggest the following areas of emphasis: the care and maintenance of collections; governance, policy and planning; fund-raising and membership development; and public programming.

The Need for Information about Museums

A serious handicap to this commission's work has been the lack of information about museums and the museum profession. There are no reliable data on the characteristics of the museum work force, the availability of various kinds of public programming or the financial picture in American museums. We cannot compare organizational structures, nor do we know the extent of the development of policies in such areas as collections management. Even such simple information as the number, type, budget size and regional distribution of museums is not regularly maintained.

There have been two nationwide studies of museums in the past 20 years. The National Endowment for the Arts' *Museums USA* profiled approximately 1,200 museums; despite limitations in the sample size and composition, the resulting report, published in 1974, contains the most definitive information we have. In 1979 the Institute of Museum Services sponsored the Museum Universe Survey, which provided useful data about the number of museums and their distribution by size, region, budget size and attendance; that study has not been updated.

In the course of our work we repeatedly felt the lack of reliable, up-to-date, quantitative and qualitative data that would help us assess the extent of the museum community's needs and formulate recommendations for the future. A profile of the museum profession would have many internal uses. Equally important is the value of such data in describing the characteristics and needs of museums to the public, the media and public and private funding sources.

Examples of the kinds of information that would be useful are:

- An economic profile of museums (endowment and budget size, sources of financial support);
- A profile of museums by discipline, budget size and geographic distribution;
- Information about the size and composition of the museum work force (including volunteers) and boards of trustees;
- Data about salary and benefit structures, presented in a way that accommodates the variability that exists throughout the museum community;
- Indicators of the effectiveness of the museum as organization (extent of exhibitions, other public programming and scholarly activity, nature of collections care and maintenance, fiscal trends);
- Projections of financial needs, both short- and long-term.

◆ RECOMMENDATION 13: Through the appropriate professional organizations or a collaboration among them, the museum community must set up a permanent mechanism for collecting, analyzing and disseminating data about museums— their numbers and locations, their facilities and finances, their personnel and trustees, their activities and attendance. Policy makers both inside and outside the museum field must have current and comprehensive data on the museum field to guide their decisions. The availability of this information will aid all who strive to meet the needs of museums and communicate both the needs and the services of these important institutions to others.

5 The Collaborative Spirit

Washington, D.C., abounds with great museums, but many of them are nowhere near the Smithsonian-lined Mall that is such familiar museum territory to residents and tourists alike. In the Dupont Circle–Kalorama neighborhood of the city, seven of these museums have formed a new consortium to promote the lesser-known riches of their collections and programs. A handsome brochure guides visitors on a walking tour of the neighborhood and its museums, and there are plans for cooperative programming, too.

Eight large science-technology museums noted for the excellence of their public programs were feeling the pressure of rising exhibition costs. Rather than compromise the quality or the quantity of their services, they formed the Science Museum Exhibit Collaborative. It will produce eight "hands-on" traveling exhibits over five years, at an average cost of $250,000 each, on topics ranging from genetic engineering to robotics. The museums share the expense and will share the exhibitions. Their joint resources will make it possible for them to continue their timely, high-quality service to the public.

In San Antonio an art museum, a science-technology/transportation museum and a history/natural history museum all operate under the administrative umbrella of the San Antonio Museum Association in an intriguing experiment in collaboration. Operations and programs are centralized; staff responsible for collections, education, exhibitions, administrative services, public relations and development serve all three museums, but each has its own director and curatorial staff.

In any number of ways, museums need and can benefit from collaboration. Although a certain measure of cooperation among institutions—jointly sponsored traveling exhibitions or sharing ideas through professional networks, for example—is common, the interlinking these three projects exemplify is a recent development. Each group of museums was able to achieve certain objectives most effectively and efficiently by working together. The Washington museums are promoting themselves more aggressively; the science museums are able to mount important exhibitions; and the San Antonio museums have a streamlined, cost-effective operation.

Gordon Ambach has spoken forcefully about the need for collaboration. At the 1980 annual meeting of the American Association of Museums, the New York state commissioner of education suggested that it was time for museums to join together for their own benefit and the benefit of their constituents. "Can we," he asked, "take a fresh look at our resources and find new patterns to take full advantage of these resources?"

At the time, economics seemed the most logical reason to set aside competition in favor of collaboration. And there is no denying the economic utility of joint efforts. Certainly, the need to use financial resources more effectively was one motivation for all three collaborations we have described. As more is written about social change in America since the 1960s, however, it is clear that collaboration is not just a matter of financial expediency. It is a new strategy that is going to change the way the affairs of both individuals and organizations are conducted. The emergence of networks and coalitions is a major trend, stemming from a changing world view of how people can most responsibly use resources. Collaborative efforts among institutions or organizations can offer mutual support and enrichment. Done cor-

Collaboration and New Museums

The National Center of Afro-American Artists and the Museum of Fine Arts in Boston have enjoyed a remarkable collaboration for more than 15 years—a collaboration that has been a partnership with clear benefits for both institutions. In 1968 Elma Lewis, artistic director of the national center, began talking with trustees of the Museum of Fine Arts about establishing a museum devoted to the collection and exhibition of paintings, prints and graphics by Afro-American artists. By early the next year the two institutions had agreed in principle to a relationship in which the MFA would supply technical and professional expertise to develop the new museum, while the center would share its special knowledge of African and Afro-American art and artists to help the larger institution broaden its programs and audience.

The Museum of the National Center of Afro-American Artists was officially established in 1969. In the early years it turned to the MFA to handle borrowing, lending and insurance matters related to mounting exhibitions. Later the museum hired a registrar trained at the MFA to manage its collections. In 1980 the museum moved to its own permanent building. It is no longer a dependent entity, but like other small, specialized museums, it still has needs it cannot meet and continues to rely on the MFA for access to exhibition hardware, design and conservation services, and technical guidance and expertise.

During the 15-year collaboration, the MFA has also benefited from the relationship. With the guidance of the national center's museum, the MFA has produced eight exhibitions of Afro-American and African art. Together the museums have developed education activities and performing arts events related to black cultural life. In an extensive new program now being planned by the education departments of the two institutions, students will visit both the MFA and the Museum of the National Center of Afro-American Artists to learn about American history and art.

This remarkable relationship continues to flourish because it is based on mutual respect and reciprocal benefits. Both institutions are dedicated to quality programming, and each comes to the partnership with an important need to be met and a special contribution to make.

rectly, collaboration enhances the ability of each participant and provides a unified, focused mechanism for achieving individual goals.

The trend is evident in all parts of society, among interest groups and institutions alike and different. It is reflected in corporate infrastructures, where managers are discovering that decentralized small units working together are more efficient than traditional hierarchies—one manifestation of the "proliferation of voices" described in chapter 1. In electoral politics the power of special interest groups and coalitions is indisputable. Among museums, there is now a closer sense of community and a clearer recognition of ties to other institutions in society. With the collaborative spirit they have already demonstrated, museums could emerge as leaders in the trend toward unified actions.

These efforts are just beginning, however. Museums in our monitoring system report only limited collaborative activity. Nearly one-quarter do no more than routine cooperative work with other local museums. Most described one or two joint projects, typically with schools, universities, performing and visual arts organizations and community groups.

One staff member characterized his museum's collaborative activity this way: "We collaborate with others regarding schedules with the intention of avoiding conflicts. We try to collaborate within the limits of our time and policy, but there is really not much collaboration." At the other end of the spectrum, a small historical society reported planning joint programs with schools, archeological clubs, the genealogical society and the local chapter of the DAR.

Since our first meeting, this commission has recognized the necessity of the collaborative spirit to the future health of museums. That view has been continually reinforced. At the San Francisco open forum, Susan Brown of the Mexican-American Legal Defense and Education Fund called for meaningful collaboration between large, established museums and smaller ethnic and racial minority museums. At the same meeting Watson M. Laetsch, vice-chancellor of the University of California, Berkeley, urged museums to work more closely with institutions of higher education, especially in planning programs for undergraduates. At other meetings the commission was reminded that collaborative television programming can help carry the museum's message. Tedwilliam Theodore, executive director of the Center for

New Television in Chicago, and Chiz Schultz, executive producer for Children's Television Workshop in New York City, encouraged museums to offer their expertise and resources to cable and broadcast television.

We see two promising avenues for collaborative efforts in the future: collaboration among individual museums, and between museums and other "independent sector" institutions.

Collaboration among Museums

The community of museums, in its infinite diversity, is in itself a successful collaboration, involving a firm commitment to reaching mutually beneficial goals without sacrificing individual concerns. The goals vary, from agreement on professional standards and ethics to a broad understanding of what it means to be a museum to the advocacy of specific interests and financial needs.

Museum professionals and organizations within the community are actively engaged in collaboration, too, in much the same spirit. Groups of museum educators, for example, meet to share ideas and sponsor joint activities that enhance their professional development. On a larger scale, state, regional and national organizations of museums and museum disciplines are important networks. Few would argue that one of the primary benefits of a professional meeting is the opportunity to know and learn from colleagues. This sense of collegiality is a particular strength of the museum profession.

Individual museums are also joining together, with increasing competence, to make their mutual needs more visible, to solve their common problems and to serve their constituencies more effectively. In the course of our work we have encountered impressive joint efforts undertaken by museums with similar interests or in close proximity to one another. Ranging from the traditional to the adventurous, these efforts include jointly organized traveling exhibitions, cooperative public relations and marketing activities and even combined fund-raising campaigns. The cooperative conservation centers described in chapter 2 are also a form of collaboration.

The collaborative spirit is both a product of the connections among museums and a connecting

International Partnerships among Museums

The nature of museum collections makes relations with other nations an integral part of museum work. Many American museums have regular ties with museums and museum professionals in other countries. International Partnerships among Museums, a special program of the American Association of Museums and the International Council of Museums, fosters international cooperation and the sharing of information among museums throughout the world. It offers museum professionals from America a chance to visit and work in a foreign museum for six weeks; then the American museum plays host to a member of the overseas museum's staff. Only three years old, the program is already enormously popular. Last year, 66 American museums, with prospective partners in 28 foreign countries, applied for participation; only 14 could be accepted.

One such exchange enhanced cooperation between the Museum of the National Center of Afro-American Artists in Boston and the National Gallery of Jamaica in Kingston. Over the years the two institutions had collaborated in presenting exhibitions of works from Africa, Afro-America and the Caribbean. The partnerships program made possible a special exhibition in Boston of works from the National Gallery of Jamaica and gave a Jamaican curator a strong background in Afro-American art in preparation for her gallery's planned expansion in that field.

The Monaghan County Museum in the Republic of Ireland was interested in the development of regional museums in the United States, and especially in the museum's role in preserving regional identity through a strong relationship to its community. Its staff also wanted to learn more about exhibition techniques and volunteerism. A partnership with Old Sturbridge Village made that learning possible. Sturbridge, for its part, gained exposure to the unique regional museum structure of Ireland.

The Arusha Museum, a branch of the National Museum of Tanzania, had a history of cooperation with the Lowie Museum of Anthropology at the University of California, Berkeley, but wanted its curator to have some firsthand experience in American museum operations. What he learned during his exchange about conservation and general museological practices benefited the entire Tanzanian museum community. At the same time the Lowie strengthened its ties with a museum in an area of the world significant to its research and exhibition interests.

Results reported by the institutions and their staff participants suggest that International Partnerships among Museums has worked very well. Each of the 21 pairs of partners plans continued collaboration in the form of joint research, exchange of staff and technical information, loan exhibitions and other activities. The sustained relationship between the Louisiana State Museum in New Orleans and the Musée du Nouveau Monde in La Rochelle, France, is particularly impressive. While strikingly dissimilar in size and scope, the two institutions share a heritage. This compatibility led them to develop *The Sun King*, a special exhibition on Louis XIV drawn from French collections; it opened in New Orleans during the 1984 World's Fair and will travel to American and French museums.

mechanism, and it promises to grow in the future. Particularly fruitful possibilities exist in educational programming, the use of equipment and facilities, income-producing ventures, media and information management technology, collections-related activities and improved public relations.

In the development of educational programs and materials, museums should do more than share ideas. Successful programs are just beginning to be replicated for use by museums with similar collections and programmatic goals. HERP lab, a series of "hands-on" activities for adults and children, makes a visit to the reptile house at the Smithsonian Institution's National Zoological Park a special event. The zoo is developing materials about the program for use by other zoos interested in providing similar participatory activities. A consortium of nine science museums across the country recently shared in the cost of an educational exhibit using the Franklin Institute Science Museum's gravity well, which was refurbished in the process. On a larger scale, three recent publications exemplify the collaborative spirit among museum educators. *Museums, Adults and the Humanities, The Art Museum as Educator* and *Museums, Magic and Children* describe successful programs and serve as planning guides.

The joint acquisition of equipment and use of facilities are partnerships motivated by economics. Sharing in expenditures may make the purchase of computers, conservation laboratory equipment or materials for exhibit production possible when a museum might not by itself be able to afford the capital outlay. Sharing space can be both economical and convenient. In Roanoke, Virginia, the Roanoke Museum of Fine Arts, the Roanoke Valley Science Museum and the Roanoke Transportation Museum occupy a cultural center with other arts institutions. The Children's Museum and the Computer Museum in Boston share a rehabilitated warehouse on Museum Wharf.

Joint ventures to produce earned income, in which a group of museums contributes to the venture capital, are worth consideration. In Minneapolis four cultural institutions contributed $2.5 million each in endowment funds to a joint investment portfolio. The McKnight Foundation matched the funds, doubling the annual return for each investor. Since earned income from programs, services and investments will be a necessary part of every museum's future financial picture, collaborative projects that use the assets of several museums—and spread the risk—should be studied.

Collaborative development of information systems for collections has many advantages. Museums should not plan computerized collections record keeping in isolation. Collaboration—or at least the sharing of plans for systems development—could keep incompatibility among systems to a minimum. Dozens of museums now use SELGEM, the Smithsonian Institution's software package, which was developed with the special needs of museums in mind. The Art Museum Association of America is now testing ARTIS, a shared software development program for collections and financial management.

Collaborative efforts in activities related to museum collections offer great opportunity for the future. Institutions with living collections routinely coordinate both acquisition and research efforts. The San Diego and the Bronx zoos, for example, recently joined to purchase a pair of rare Russian horses. Art museums like those in the Washington State Print Consortium, a group of small and medium-sized museums, are buying art together and sharing the responsibility of care and the privilege of exhibiting. Even museums with large acquisition budgets are beginning to pool their resources. The J. Paul Getty Museum and the Norton Simon Museum jointly own paintings. The National Portrait Gallery and the Museum of Fine Arts, Boston, share ownership of the Gilbert Stuart portraits of George and Martha Washington.

Collaborative public relations activities are already common among museums and successful in raising community and tourist awareness of local institutions. Joint promotion has more impact, is more economical and presents a more unified image for a museum than can separate campaigns. There are collaborative public relations efforts in the Brandywine River Valley (Pennsylvania and Delaware), Boston, Rochester, New York, Washington, D.C., and Indianapolis. A stretch of Fifth Avenue in New York City has been dubbed "Museum Mile" by an organization formed to promote the museums between 82nd Street and 105th Streets.

Museums and the Culture Industry

As recently as 1979, the museums in Rochester, New York, had little joint programming. Today the picture has changed dramatically, thanks to Museums of Rochester (MOR), an association of public relations directors from local museums.

Following the examples of the Museums of Boston (MOB), the Brandywine Valley museums in Pennsylvania and Delaware and Museum Mile in New York City, the museums of Rochester joined together in 1980 to increase public awareness of their institutions as valuable cultural resources. With the support of the museums' directors, the first Sunday in May was designated Museum Day, with free admission and shuttle transportation to all museums. Under the sponsorship of Eastman Kodak Company, the event is now annual, bringing thousands of visitors to Rochester's museums.

Once they saw what they could do by working together, the public relations directors expanded their activities beyond building public awareness to demonstrating the economic impact museums have on the city and showing civic leaders the contribution cultural resources can make. In the four years since MOR was founded, each of the participating museums has experienced increased attendance, scholars study their collections more frequently and museum facilities are used more often for meetings and other events. A "museum trail" marks the way to all museums, and local hotels sometimes give their guests tickets to museums.

In 1982 MOR did an economic impact study to give city leaders information about the purchasing power of museums and the amount of money generated locally by museum employees and museum visitors. As a result, other groups began to understand how cultural institutions can help city promotion. Through the Rochester-Monroe County Convention and Visitor Bureau, a Visitor Industry Committee was established; today it includes more than 100 representatives from the city's museums, hotels, many restaurants, recreational attractions and other visitor service organizations.

As a collective form of community outreach, MOR has given community leaders a direct way to communicate with the museums. MOR members have even joined city officials in testifying before state government bodies on the effects of travel on the city. Rochester now has a strong presence at tour industry meetings, and museums have been central in that achievement. Mary Kay Ingenthron, deputy director for public affairs at the Strong Museum, explains that museums and other cultural institutions "are one of the primary reasons for people to stop in Rochester—you can get a hotel anywhere."

Rochester's museums are pleased with their role in increasing the visibility of cultural resources and in their work with other cultural facilities, recreational attractions, hotels and restaurants. Their individual identities have remained intact, and the success of their collaborative efforts has prompted two new museum organizations. The Museums of Rochester-Educators (MORE) now meets monthly, while the Rochester Area Museum Directors meets quarterly to discuss upcoming plans for individual institutions. In Rochester collaboration thrives, and everybody benefits.

Extending the Collaborative Spirit

Sharing Educational Programs

In a society that fosters competition, museums thrive on sharing their collections and programs. The Exploratorium in San Francisco—a pioneer in the development of interactive exhibits—is known throughout the world for its ingenious, effective museum displays. Are these exhibits prepared behind closed doors, their formulas patented secrets? Just the opposite. A grant from the Kellogg Foundation is supporting a program that enables museums around the country to learn about Exploratorium exhibit techniques.

Frank Oppenheimer, Exploratorium director, is dedicated to the idea that exhibits should be not only approachable and fascinating; they must also teach. Through its Dissemination Program, his museum teaches other museums as well. Now in its fifth and final year, the program includes internships, conferences and publications. Again this year, several groups of museum professionals will come to the Exploratorium for two-week internships. As in the past, these interns will work closely with each other and with the museum's staff, studying the exhibits and discussing possibilities for their own institutions. More than 100 people from nearly 75 museums have been able to get to know the Exploratorium in this way, and to carry home its ideas and approaches.

Conferences on topics such as science and the media and the elements of good exhibit design have reached another 250 people. The conference on science and the media brought together representatives from television, newspapers, magazines, book publishing and libraries, as well as scientists from museums, universities and colleges. Discussions focused on the strengths of each medium and its potential for presenting information about science to the public. A loose network still operates today among the participants, who share the goal of increasing public understanding of science.

The Dissemination Program's publications have reached the greatest numbers by far. In the past four years the museum has produced two "cookbooks" describing how its exhibits are prepared and how they might be duplicated in other museums. In all, 135 exhibits have been shared in this fashion—and they are appearing in museums around the world.

For the future, the Exploratorium is investigating how it might continue the internship program beyond the period of grant support and extend its study of exhibit development. With new exhibits on language and perception, the museum has expanded into the humanities. Staff members believe there are common elements among all types of museums with regard to the nature of learning from objects and strategies for developing educational exhibits. Articulating, and then sharing, those common elements will be the next step in the Exploratorium's tradition of collaboration.

In this commission's exploration of challenges and opportunities for the future, we invited the participation of a number of people from outside the museum world. Some represented business, government or the media, but what many had in common with museums was their involvement in America's "independent sector"—that multifaceted group of nonprofit educational, cultural, religious, community service, political and social organizations and institutions devoted to the public welfare.

Waldemar Nielsen describes the independent sector as a balance between government and business. The "untidy but wonderfully exuberant" institutions that constitute it provide, he says, both tangible services and a less tangible but no less important humanizing influence in our lives. The existence of the independent sector ensures the "continuing responsiveness, creativity and self-renewal of our democratic society."

On the basis of what we heard from participants, we know that the independent sector is ready for new collaborative efforts. The commission process itself helped establish a new network with them that may well be one of the most valuable products of our work. When carried out with the best interests of each partner in mind, joint projects between museums and other organizations can help create a stronger public presence for cultural institutions and a fuller public understanding of their importance to American life.

We found a natural link of purpose between museums and performing and visual arts organizations, libraries, elementary and secondary schools, universities and colleges, continuing education programs, parks and recreation departments and preservation groups. Collaboration among cultural and educational institutions can make them a more effective force and bring recognition to the value of their contribution to community life.

Partnerships between museums and schools and universities are some of the most longstanding joint efforts in which museums have been involved. Chapter 3 of this report discusses the museum-school relationship. With universities, the most familiar form of collaboration is in graduate and undergraduate training programs for museum work. There are intriguing possibilities for cooperative public programs; a good example is the computer van cosponsored by the Space Center in Alamogordo, New Mexico, and New Mexico State University, which brings computer instruction to school districts throughout the state.

Cooperative lobbying efforts are a more recent development. Coalitions of arts and humanities organizations, such as the National Humanities Alliance and the American Arts Alliance, work for the interests of their constituencies. The American Association of Museums has worked closely with other arts organizations and libraries to promote legislation giving artists and authors an income tax deduction for the donation of their work to charitable organizations. On other income tax issues, the AAM has allied with universities.

This kind of collaboration is also occurring at the state and local levels. In New York State, the Coalition of Living Museums promotes the importance of institutions with living collections. In many cities and states, from Philadelphia to Texas, cultural alliances serve a variety of purposes—lobbying, staff training and technical assistance, marketing and promotion of member organizations and sharing of services to minimize costs.

The relationship between museums and libraries, so close in the early years of their development, is being renewed in many communities. The Great Plains Experience, a project funded by the National Endowment for the Humanities, brought libraries and museums together in seven projects designed to foster appreciation for regional history. Performing and visual arts organizations sometimes share space or equipment with museums; the Guthrie Theater adjoining the Walker Art Center in Minneapolis and the theater of the Virginia Museum of Fine Arts, Richmond, are two well-known examples. And cultural institutions are beginning to experiment with collaborative fund-raising activities, too.

Partnerships with other independent sector organizations are less common, perhaps because the link of purpose is not as clear as with cultural and educational institutions. The common ground between museums and community organizations is their capacity to contribute in a broad way to the quality of human life, so the basis for collaboration among them is the stimulation of mutual support and enrichment of purpose, the use of one another's resources and the promotion of a shared belief that their separate contributions form a meaningful whole. Collaboration with

Joint Expeditions

Museums form collections in very different ways—through gifts, bequests or purchases, by acquiring objects individually and in groups. Natural history museums, botanical gardens and zoos send scientists into the field to collect the specimens their staffs will use for research and exhibitions.

These expeditions are sometimes collaborative efforts organized by a large institution and involving others of varying sizes. The largest multi-institutional project ever attempted is now under way in Venezuela. With funds from the National Geographic Society and the National Science Foundation, the Missouri Botanical Garden and the New York Botanical Garden have organized an expedition to study the flora and fauna of the Cerro de la Neblina region of Venezuela. Nearly 80 scientists from institutions including the University of Michigan, the Smithsonian Institution, Vanderbilt University and Florida State University are combing this unexplored area in a project that will take one full year or more to complete.

A project of this scope requires careful planning by the host country. Venezuela's Ministry of Environment, a division of the National Park Institute, provided the permit for exploration. Funds were made available through the country's Academy of Natural Science, Mathematics and Physics. Equally important were the local arrangements. As a participant in the early phases of the expedition pointed out, "Logistics can make or break a project like this. Early on, for instance, the helicopter that was being used was in ill repair. Much time was lost because of equipment failure." A new helicopter allowed the project to continue on schedule.

Work began in January 1984 and will continue at least until December. Approximately 20 scientists are in the region at a time, working for several weeks or months before they are replaced by a new group. The scientists collect sets of at least five specimens of plants and animals. One set stays in Venezuela, the plants becoming part of the collections of the National Herbarium in Caracas. The other sets are distributed among the other institutions sponsoring the expedition. In this way, scientists are gathering and recording important data about the unexplored mountain region as well as adding to the inventories of their own institutions.

The advantages of collaborative expeditions are not limited to the sharing of expenses, labor and specimens for collections. The quality of the expedition team is enhanced by the participation of a variety of institutions, each of which assigns its best scientists to the project.

community organizations serves museums well because it fortifies the notion that they have a serious service function, that they indeed meet a human need.

Museums should seek mutually beneficial ways to work with citizen action groups, women's organizations, health and social welfare organizations, service clubs and other community groups. This effort is a new dimension to outreach, and the results can be productive for all involved. Programs that bring the museum experience to a wider audience are often planned and carried out by the museum alone, but they could be joint endeavors, as some museums are already demonstrating. At the Boston Children's Museum, a work program for disadvantaged teenagers, called Kids at Risk, is designed in conjunction with the schools, the criminal justice system and social service organizations. The planning process for the new St. Louis Science Center involved advisory committees with representatives from public and private schools, local universities, corporations and the scientific community. In cooperation with civic organizations, many museums have begun to offer volunteer opportunities for senior citizens.

The museum community needs more collaboration that strengthens its ties to the rest of society. Partnerships with service organizations are, in fact, a key to an active, vital future role for museums. Whenever human needs are addressed, cultural needs must be on the agenda. Collaboration between museums and community organizations can advance the services museums provide.

◆ RECOMMENDATION 14: In a world of diminishing resources, collaboration among museums and between museums and other organizations will be increasingly obligatory. Rather than opting for joint programs through necessity, museums must take the lead in such efforts, for they offer many benefits in addition to economic efficiency. Collaboration can enhance the effectiveness and community visibility of museums. In their endeavor to meet the future positively, we urge that museums actively seek ways of working together and with other community organizations.

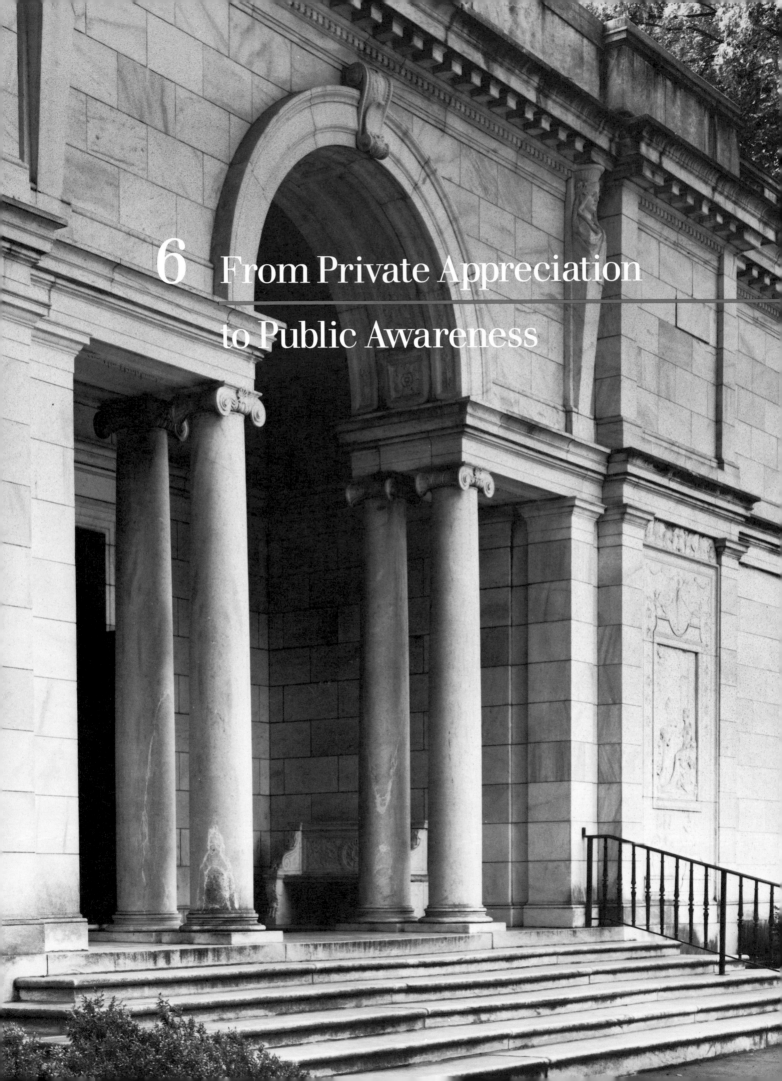

6 From Private Appreciation to Public Awareness

There is no doubt that museums have intensely personal meanings to a great many people. Again and again, this commission has encountered a deep private appreciation for individual museums, their collections and the multifaceted museum experience. No two people feel the same way about museums, and no two sets of impressions have the same origins. But the rich personal meanings with which museums are endowed are curiously unrelated to their collective public image, an image often encumbered by clichés.

Tradition prescribes a staid and understated countenance for museums, and the museum community too readily accepts it. The stereotyped museum is a collection of old objects, with musty corridors where things never change and one can only whisper. For many, museums are elitist institutions where they think they would be uncomfortable. For others, museums are just a refuge from rainy days and dull Sunday afternoons.

But none of these clichés rings true. Today's museums are lively gathering places, filled with imaginative exhibits and bustling with visitors. There are lectures, workshops, live performances, "hands-on" activities and always the real things on display. Public spaces with orientation galleries, restaurants and shops are designed to welcome visitors and make them comfortable. Behind the scenes, the complex machinery that enables museums to study, preserve and explain the nation's cultural heritage is constantly in motion.

During the commission process, we asked a variety of people to tell us about their feelings for museums, and the responses were just as diverse as the respondents. All of them, though, testified to the affection people feel for their favorite museums. A young girl who lived just two blocks from the Metropolitan Museum of Art spent her spare time as a teenager in the French period rooms and decided on a career in museum work. A woman new to a community in Florida felt at home after she began working as a volunteer in a small archeological museum. A scientist credits the American Museum of Natural History with the inspiration for his education and life's work. A retired physician began collecting prints and drawings through interest in his daughter's work as a curator. "If science makes life possible," he reflected, "art makes life livable."

These experiences are multiplied across the country and echoed among museum goers of all ages. Why, then, is there such a gap between, on the one hand, the nature of museums and the private affection they engender and, on the other, the stereotypical public image? The disparity is at least in part due to the unwillingness or inability of museum professionals to engage in image building on behalf of museums. But museums have too great a stake in the public's image of them, and too important a responsibility for service, to languish because of a reluctance to promote themselves. This reluctance must be overcome. It is time for the museum community to take an active role in shaping the public image of museums by modernizing the stereotypes and turning individual private affection into broad public awareness and support.

The public must begin to see museums as institutions essential for civilized life. Edgar Preston Richardson has described the challenge: "What is missing from the museum world of North America," he says, "is an educated adult comprehension of the immense and fascinating treasures of art, science and history assembled in our museums." People need to know more about museums; they should understand both the multitude of functions museums undertake and the vast variety of the objects, artifacts and specimens in the

Private Memories and Personal Experiences

Just mention the word "museum," and your friends are likely to recall a favorite museum, a well-loved object or a memorable experience. Some people arrive at career choices through museums; others claim their lives have been changed by encounters with these institutions. The commission collected unsolicited personal tributes to museums and asked people at open forums—visitors, museum staff members, trustees and volunteers—what museums meant to them. Some examples:

▪ A woman told us about moving to a new community and "knowing not a soul." A neighbor introduced her to the director of the local museum, and through the museum she "found a new life." As she put it, "I've been a volunteer and served in many capacities in this fine small archeological museum all these years. Education is the hope of America, and an interesting museum experience can last a lifetime."

▪ The director of a well-known children's museum told us that she spent her spare time as a teenager "escaping to the world of rococo fantasy" in the French period rooms at the Metropolitan Museum of Art. It is not surprising, she said, that when she graduated from college, museum work was what she wanted to do. "Being exposed all those years to the *real* things has certainly influenced my thinking about what museums can mean to a child's interior life."

▪ Another young woman's museum experience had a ripple effect. After taking an art history class at the Philadelphia Museum of Art, she began oil painting but did not pursue it. As she tells it, "My mother retrieved my supplies and began painting herself. Shortly after this, she became ill, and found painting a great comfort as she dealt with her pain. When she died, family members were able to have her artworks as a remembrance."

▪ Representative Sidney R. Yates (D-Ill.) paid tribute to museums not only on behalf of himself, but for his grandchildren as well. He said: "Last summer I visited the Grand Teton National Park with my grandchildren, who are nine and six. They had grown up frequenting the Field Museum and the Adler Planetarium in Chicago. I looked on in wonder as they identified various plants and animals, and at night, under the starry sky, I listened with awe as they pointed out Jupiter, Venus, Saturn, Andromeda, the Big Bear and other constellations. And as I watched them, I thought how wonderful was this wedding of Chicago's museums and this beautiful national park in fulfilling our needs for learning and enjoyment."

aggregate museum collection that is our nation's common wealth. They should know that the permanence and authority of museums—important elements in their traditional image—do not imply stasis, for institutions can be both permanent and lively, authoritative and forward thinking. Surely museum professionals, who are so skilled at enlightening the public and stimulating their understanding of both the concrete and the abstract, can do a more effective job of image making for American museums. They need to explain and promote the distinctive contributions of museums in an enterprising way. We have described those contributions in this report as the starting point for what we hope will be a clearer, more positive public image for our institutions.

In some respects, it is a matter of marketing, an idea some museums have only recently begun to accept. Others are already setting high standards in this activity. Many promotional projects have short-term goals—to enroll new members, publicize a special exhibition, draw tourists to the museum. While these are important, and often effective, museums need to take the longer view, too. Marketing as a consistent effort builds a foundation of public understanding and appreciation. Over time, the public learns about the values on which museums are founded, the heritage they collect, the knowledge they embody and the services they perform. In turn, with greater understanding, the public will use and support museums more fully.

Museums need to invite the public to become more fully involved in their mission. Most people have a limited appreciation of what museums are all about; they remember the largest dinosaur, the oldest mummy, the newest space capsule. If the museum includes them, however, in all of its activities and programs, beyond the single visit, they will feel themselves partners of the museum, not just observers. Their experience will be so much the richer.

Museums will benefit, too. A stronger involvement by the public in the mission of museums will naturally lead to a stronger and more reliable base of financial support. In fact, it would be risky to seek increased financial backing without first stimulating a deeper public commitment. Without it, no amount of financial support can be strong or reliable.

The public perception of museums today is incomplete in several respects. People should recognize, first, the central role museums collectively

Marketing Museums

"You Can Feel the Fun," "Be a FONZ," "Fireworks at Christmas," and "Project Pink"—all catchy phrases, all memorable and all part of museum marketing programs. Bold banners fly above the doorways of art museums announcing exhibitions; city buses carry placards with information about museum programs and hours; and advertisements appear in newspapers, magazines and on television. Museums have begun to take marketing seriously, and the results are impressive.

The Memphis Museums, Inc., for example, recently launched Project Pink, the first major membership recruitment effort ever conducted in a mid-South museum system. The object of the campaign is to increase membership by making the community more aware of the services the museums provide. The campaign's title comes from one of the museums in the group, the Memphis Pink Palace Museum. In April 1982, the museum merged with two other museum-related institutions—Magevney House and Lichterman Nature Center—to expand area opportunities for enjoyment and education. The merger also led to the marketing campaign that invited people to "join in the three-for-all."

Project Pink is a three-year membership development program that is expected to bring in 7,500 individual, family, student and patron members, as well as 250 corporate and business members, by June 1986. The project's communication plan includes outdoor advertising, television and radio public service announcements and a 100,000-piece direct mail campaign. Materials are simple but striking. Brochures, buttons and bumper stickers all have the same look, with the words "Project Pink" always — naturally — in pink.

The campaign includes the usual appeal to individuals but also targets corporate and student members. For corporations,

the museum builds on the fact that the personal lives of employees are important to their job satisfaction. It offers companies a way to demonstrate concern for employees and their families by purchasing memberships that include a host of privileges, such as a special planetarium show for employees and scholarships for education department programs. The project also includes Project Pink—For Kids Only. Students are invited to join the museum through the mail or at school, and the school with the highest number of student memberships wins a computer.

Project Pink is getting results. It is clear to the community that the museum board has formally accepted responsibility for the long-range development of the three institutions under its direction. Programming at the museums has expanded, and both attendance and membership have grown. The number of individual members has risen from 250 in 1979 to more than 2,000 in 1981—the first year of the campaign. In 1983 individual membership grew again to 3,250, and with its current campaign the museum projects 5,000 members by 1985. There were no corporate members when Project Pink began; today there are 120. Attendance has also increased. At the Pink Palace Museum, for instance, annual attendance has gone from 97,965 in 1978 to 210,879 in 1983.

The museums recently received a special award from the Tennessee Association of Museums for their exemplary marketing project. But Project Pink is much more than a membership drive. Memphis Museums, Inc., wants to serve its community better. As a result of good marketing the people of Memphis know about the many services their museums offer— and they use them more fully.

play in preserving our heritage. More specifically, they should know that caring for objects is a complex and critical task. The museums they visit would not exist were it not for the detailed technical processes of research, care and documentation. People should realize, too, that behind the scenes in museums there are skilled professionals responsible for all they see when they visit, and much they do not see. A museum is not just static objects; it is a human enterprise, inside and out. The public needs to know about the significant role museums play in American education and in scholarly research. Finally, people need to be more aware that a visit to a museum can be an individual and pleasurable learning experience, a way to explore and expand horizons freely.

To ensure the broadest kind of public service and the broadest base of financial support, the museum community must begin now to build an appropriate collective image. Individually, museums need to promote the services they offer. Together, museums must clarify what they are and what they contribute to the quality of life. The substance of this message—and the foundation for a new public image—is found in the pages of this report. It is now up to museums and the museum community to transmit the message. We suggest two audiences: opinion leaders and public officials, and the general public.

Sending the Message to Opinion Leaders and Public Officials

The political advocacy skills the museum community has acquired in the past decade will be useful in furnishing opinion leaders and public officials with a complete picture of contemporary museums and the services they provide. Organized lobbying activities have given museums a strong presence on the federal scene and, in many cases, at the state and local levels. Now, with this commission's report in hand, museums are well equipped to begin more broad-based advocacy efforts that will give elected officials and leaders in the public and private sectors a fuller understanding of what museums mean to our society.

Until the late 1970s, political advocacy in the museum world was isolated but earnest. With the growth of federal support for the arts, science and the humanities, though, came the need to articulate what the federal role should be in relation to museums. Since the AAM's Legislative Program was inaugurated in 1979, museums have joined together to become visible, effective participants in the political process. Museum professionals, through their professional associations, have combined forces to make the mission, needs and interests of museums known and understood in the public policy arena and to lobby on specific issues.

Organized political activity has prevented funding to museums from being curtailed in a political atmosphere that favors a decreased role for government. Concerted lobbying efforts by museum professionals on behalf of the Institute of Museum Services, for example, have twice saved it from extinction. During the past year, the care and maintenance needs of museum collections have received special attention in Congress because the museum community has informed key representatives and senators about the critical nature of those needs.

There are parallel activities at the state and local levels. Formally and informally, museums now band together on issues that affect them. In a few states museums have used their own lobbyists in the state legislature—sometimes to represent them on special issues and sometimes on a continuing basis. State arts and humanities alliances are also effective advocacy bases for museums. As a result of the new political sophistication acquired by museums, public officials know more about their needs and the reasons for those needs.

On the local level, museums that receive municipal and county support must work consistently to involve public officials and promote the importance of their institutions. Here there are strong specific arguments to be made for the value of museums as amenities. In addition to their direct economic impact as business enterprises, museums and other cultural institutions enhance the quality of life in a community; as part of the package of amenities, they encourage business activity, stimulate private investment and strengthen the local image.

The museum community's success at lobbying dispels some myths museum people hold about themselves and their institutions. Museums, diverse as they are, can have a unified voice. In fact, the increase in political activity has propelled museums to coalesce more firmly around the concerns they do hold in common—the care of collections, for example, or the importance of the charitable deduction as a stimulus for financial

Public Awareness through Advocacy

Political advocacy skills are serving the museum community well at all levels of government. As museum professionals become more adept at describing the assets and needs of museums, public officials are responding. At the state level, coalitions representing a range of cultural interests have been very successful. One example is the Texas Arts Alliance (TAA), whose purpose is to focus public attention on the importance of the arts and the needs of arts institutions, to encourage donations and allocations of funds to the arts and to work with other statewide institutions having similar goals. Alliance members include institutions, museum professionals and interested individuals such as artists and trustees.

Informing state legislators about the financial needs of the cultural and arts communities is one element of the alliance's program. Observers of the political scene in Austin witnessed a polished lobbying operation when 1,800 TAA members descended on the capitol building on February 23, 1983, designated Arts Day, and visited every state legislator. The event ended with an opportunity for constituents and representatives to gather informally at receptions held in several Austin galleries.

The focal point of the TAA's efforts is to secure increased funding for the Texas Commission on the Arts, the agency that distributes financial assistance to scores of cultural and arts organizations throughout the state. An important victory was won when the legislature appropriated $9 million for the 1984–85 biennium. With this increase, the commission has one of the fastest growth rates among all state agencies— from $1.6 million in 1978–79, to $3.4 million in 1980–81, to $4.3 million in 1982–83, to the current $9 million.

The TAA's success is grounded in solid planning and hard work. Long before Arts Day—now a biennial event—participants receive briefing materials and are invited to a special seminar on arts-related legislative issues. This preparation helps participants understand the legislative process as well as the specific state and local arts issues that affect them.

The annual Texas Arts Awards, recognizing leadership and dedication to the arts, is another alliance project. Awards are given to businesses, individual donors and artists, the media, community organizations, schools and entire communities in a ceremony held in Austin that attracts arts, cultural, civic and business leaders. To endorse the spirit of collaboration necessary for responsible arts programming, each award is presented by two people—one from the cultural community and one from business or government. The awards and the accompanying goodwill and publicity are, in the view of the alliance, an important vehicle for enhancing the visibility of the arts.

In Texas, political advocacy is working. The increasing public awareness of the importance of the arts, as well as the substantial growth in funding, are ample proof.

Promoting Public Service Organizations

For nearly a century, the American Library Association has been conducting creative and sophisticated campaigns to make the public more aware of the importance of libraries. Its most visible program is National Library Week, initiated in 1958 under the guidance of the National Book Committee, an organization of publishing house representatives. The reason for the committee's sponsorship was clear—it was to the advantage of book publishers for people to read books. When the committee disbanded in 1978, the American Library Association began its own national public awareness campaign.

Since then, the focus has shifted slightly. The ALA still promotes reading, but it emphasizes campaigns to build programs, market services and attract local support for the nation's libraries. At first ALA members were reluctant to "toot their own horn," as Peggy Barker, director of the association's Public Information Office, puts it; promotion seemed self-serving. But now they are convinced of the benefits achieved by public service organizations that speak with a loud and clear voice in their communities. They are strong proponents of active promotion as the first step toward wider use of library holdings and services.

With an annual budget of about $500,000, the ALA's Public Information Office makes a large selection of publicity materials available to member libraries at minimal cost. The ALA's 1984 campaign centered on the "Superman" theme, asserting that "Knowledge is *real* power." Eye-catching posters, bookmarks and advertisements boasted that libraries "fight the forces of ignorance and evil." The ALA provides a guide to running a publicity campaign that emphasizes promotion as a part of the overall library management strategy and explains how to make the best use of time, money and energy.

The ALA's national public awareness campaign inspires promotional activities at the state and local levels. In Pennsylvania, for instance, local library associations sponsored a successful drive to have the national library symbol included in the international manual of road signs. Some 500 signs manufactured by the Pennsylvania Department of Transportation will soon mark library locations throughout the state. In New London, New Hampshire, the Fernald Library staff at Colby-Sawyer College names a Patron of the Year—the person "singularly responsible for the greatest number of purchase orders, interlibrary loan requests and reference questions." At Stevenson House—Delaware's Juvenile Detention Center in Milford—every student signed a pledge promising "to read one book during National Library Week, and share it with a friend." The Rowan Public Library in Salisbury, North Carolina, and its local friends group sponsored a Doorway to Success essay contest, inviting patrons to explain how the library had helped them succeed.

The ALA's efforts to increase public awareness and use of library resources have caught on in the nation's libraries. Museums, too, are a public resource, and the same strategy could help tell people about the pleasures and services that museums offer.

support. Where there was once concern that involvement in the political arena would compromise the integrity of museums, it is now clear that political activity in fact ensures museums a certain independence; expressions of need and priority are best generated from within, not determined by outsiders from a distant perspective.

Museums should turn now to another kind of advocacy as a means of building a new collective public image. Not only elected officials, but community leaders, business leaders and all those who help shape public opinion must be more fully acquainted with museums. Museums must work to involve these leaders in museum activities, tell them about the basic functions and essential needs of museums, and promote museums as vital community resources. One of the intents of this report is to provide the basis for an extended advocacy effort on behalf of individual museums and the museum community at large. If the people we call "opinion leaders" are solidly behind museums and fully cognizant of the potential service of these institutions, the public will follow suit. A clearer understanding of museums on the part of opinion leaders can help broaden the museum community's political base, generate a stronger foundation of financial support and give museums the visibility they need to be used well by their constituencies.

Sending the Message to the Public

The American public is the ultimate key to a new image for museums. How people perceive museums determines how much and how well they use them and, ultimately, how fully they support them.

What does the public really know about museums? People flock to exhibitions, enjoy the environment of the buildings and grounds, appreciate the importance of introducing their children and their friends to museums. But beyond providing memorable experiences, museums keep their audiences at a distance. Few visitors know how a painting is cared for, an exhibition is conceived and assembled, a group of objects is stored. Few know how little of a museum's collection is usually on view, and how the choices are made to exhibit certain objects and not others. Few understand that museums are places where they can learn in an informal, independent way. And certainly, few know what it costs to run a museum, and why it costs so much.

The public's perception of libraries is not nearly so limited. Security requirements, the need for storage space, the importance of care in handling books, the issues of censorship and access are more familiar. The functions of libraries are more visible, so the public knows about the conditions that enable them to operate and serve their communities well. Schools teach children how libraries work and how to use them. A national campaign sponsored by the American Library Association promotes libraries as essential public services and invites people to use and enjoy their resources. As a result, libraries have always been ahead of museums on local and national agendas.

Museums, too, could invite the public to have a greater stake in them. There is a subtle but important difference between asking potential visitors, members or contributors to attend, join or support a museum, and asking them to share in its rich resources. Museums are beginning to recognize that involving people in the institution is the surest way to achieving full community appreciation of the museum's public service. Houston's Museum of Fine Arts asks members to "contribute to the fine art of running our museum." In its promotional brochure, the Southwest Museum is billed as "the best kept secret in Los Angeles. . . . And secrets like this are meant to be shared."

The process of museum work can be shared with the general public, too. People are curious about what goes on behind the scenes in museums. In recent years, some museums have made it a point to let the public know there is more to a museum than meets the eye. Conservation work is carried on in public spaces or explained in text panels accompanying exhibitions. Exhibitions explain the motives behind the formation of collections. Visitor orientation galleries describe not only the visible attractions of the museum, but all the things a museum does.

Increasing public awareness of the whole museum should not be an isolated activity but an attitude that permeates the museum's philosophy of communication with the public and the approach it takes to learning. By introducing visitors to the processes and activities that are the museum's essence, the whole museum naturally becomes part of the learning process. The aspects of museums that visitors are familiar with—special exhibitions, permanent installations, gallery talks,

A History Museum and Its Public

Housed in Rembrandt Peale's 1814 Baltimore Museum building, the Peale Museum feels a special responsibility for collecting objects that document Baltimore's past, present and future. Successful though the Peale has been, recent studies made it apparent that to most of Baltimore's citizens a history museum is still just a peculiar type of art museum—one that acquires and displays older objects selected to satisfy the taste of the connoisseur. In Baltimore this image was rooted in fact. The city's museums had strong decorative arts and painting collections representing the era before the Civil War, but little historical material, except for prints and photographs, from subsequent periods. In effect, for Baltimore's museums, history stopped in 1920.

The Peale Museum's staff recognized that to collect and preserve the city's recent past, it would need a supportive public that cared about Baltimore history. Can the 20th Century Be Saved? is a program that aims to involve Maryland and Baltimore residents in the process of identifying significant trends in 20th-century urban life—social history, technological and commercial development, communications and transportation. Through the program, the museum staff wants to encourage people to consider this century part of the historical past and to understand that history consists not only of antique furniture, prints and silver; the objects of their daily life, too, are examples of material culture.

To engage the public in a discussion of these issues, museum staff appeared on radio and television and wrote for local newspapers to describe the difficulties faced by an urban history museum charged with preserving a record of "customs and manners" for future generations. In the spring of 1984 the museum held public symposiums on "saving" the 20th century, with archeologists, historians, folklorists, collectors and museum specialists as speakers. A multimedia exhibit that traveled to shopping malls, senior centers and libraries featured a 10-minute videotape explaining the challenges in collecting contemporary objects. There were photographs of present-day Baltimore and objects already in the Peale's 20th-century collection, and visitors were asked to nominate objects they thought the museum should collect. Early choices ranged from a kaleidoscope of major sports events and figures to the neon sign atop the Domino Sugar building. All these suggestions and others will go into a new exhibit, 20th-Century Baltimore.

As part of the citywide ceremonies introducing Can the 20th Century Be Saved? students from Chinquapin Middle School interviewed residents at the Waxter Center for Senior Citizens to learn about life as a teenager half a century ago. The school librarian noted, "These students have not only had a personal experience with history, but have developed some very special relationships as well. I don't think they will ever forget the facts of these people's lives." Nor is it likely, with the Peale's effort bearing fruit in many directions, that the history of 20th-century Baltimore will be forgotten.

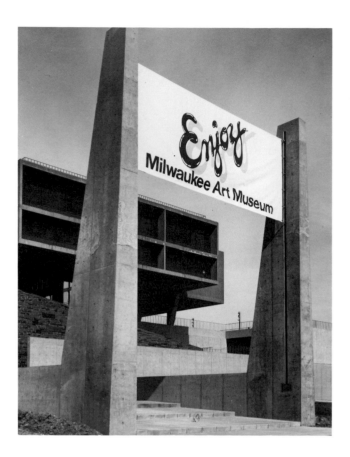

programs for schoolchildren—are appropriate mechanisms for showing how museums operate.

For their part, museums must also learn more about their audience. In addition to demographic characteristics, social science researchers now emphasize the importance of knowing about values and lifestyles. Many museums regularly conduct audience studies to discover who their visitors really are. Some museums—the Toledo Museum of Art, the Carnegie Institute in Pittsburgh, the Ohio Historical Society and a few others—have even studied the reasons people do not visit museums, and looked into ways to reach those potential audiences. The American Museum of Natural History used its audience survey as a theme for its 1983 annual report, demonstrating the important role of the public in museum operations and programming.

Museums can use this commission's report as one tool for describing museums and inviting greater public awareness and involvement. But it is time for a much broader effort on behalf of the whole museum community. Among the general public and opinion leaders alike, it is time to be more aggressive about ensuring that museums have a collective public image which is in tune with what they are today and an expansion of the individual, personal affection they engender. A new public image for museums is necessary if they are to have both the philosophical and financial support they will need to continue their essential public service into the next century.

◆ RECOMMENDATION 15: A national program should be established to strengthen the public's awareness of the value of museums and to cultivate public commitment to museums as institutions that provide essential services to society. The American Association of Museums, in cooperation with other national museum organizations, should initiate this public awareness campaign to celebrate the collective vitality of our nation's museums and encourage the public to use and support museums as community resources and sources of personal enjoyment and enlightenment.

7 The Economic Picture

A Joint Venture

In saving the topic of financial stability for the end of our report, we recall the wry realism of Ralph Waldo Emerson, who said it is always difficult to remember when times were not hard and money not scarce. When this commission first met in early 1982, museums were facing economic conditions more uncertain than those experienced in many years. The hard times were immediate, and the threats to the public-private partnership of museum support were real.

One approach for the commission would have been to react by outlining the specific financial needs of museums and proposing solutions. But responding to the immediate situation would have been a mere stopgap. We wanted instead to lay a firm groundwork for the future; we wanted to describe the assets of museums, not just enumerate their needs. To be credible and to elicit a positive, fruitful response from supporters of museums, expressions of financial need must not be crisis-oriented. They must come instead as part of a larger assertion that museums are essential national resources which not only merit but require a system of financial support in which all sectors of society participate. That has been a central theme of this commission report.

For a museum to achieve its full potential, it must work out an appropriate balance among many competing responsibilities, including a dual allegiance to its collections and its public. The most troublesome compromises museums have made in recent years have resulted from contradictory circumstances: the public's need and enthusiasm for museums have never been greater, and the resulting demands on the resources of museums has never been heavier. At the same time, for many museums, those resources are dwindling.

In early 1982, the nation was in the midst of a recession. The president had, for the second year, proposed a budget that would substantially diminish the federal government's role in support of museums. The elimination of the Institute of Museum Services and the National Science Foundation's Public Understanding of Science Program were proposed, and the National Endowments for the Arts and the Humanities were slated for substantial budget reductions. It appeared that the economic climate—in particular the erosion in federal support—would have deleterious effects on the financial commitment individuals, businesses, private foundations, and state and local governments would make to museums. And all this was happening in the face of rapidly increasing operating costs. In 1970 these expenses consumed, on the average, one-half of the budgets of most museums, while in 1980 the proportion had risen to two-thirds.

Unlike other cultural institutions, museums cannot cancel seasons or productions to save money. They cannot scale down the fixed costs related to maintaining their buildings and collections. Instead they constrict services in ways that may be imperceptible to the public, and therefore all the more threatening. They postpone conservation efforts and improvements in storage facilities. They restrict staff travel for research and in-service training. They cancel plans to publish a catalog of the collection or a scholarly monograph series. Some museums are forced to take more visible measures. They cut public programs, curtail hours to save on the cost of security and building maintenance, close some exhibit areas to the public, reduce staff. Outreach programs, experimental education programs, and activities for the elderly and the handicapped are often the first

Cause-Related Marketing

"Now everyone in Cincinnati can become a philanthropist," announced an American Express advertisement, part of a fundraising program for the Cincinnati Art Museum that raised $32,000 in three months. For American Express the partnership with the museum was an experiment in "cause-related marketing." Responding to cuts in federal funds for cultural organizations, American Express set out to help in a way that made good business sense. Its innovative program ties use of American Express services and products to direct donations to cultural institutions.

The Cincinnati Art Museum had put conservation treatment of Benjamin West's *Ophelia and Laertes* at the top of its list of needs; the painting had not been cleaned and relined since West last retouched it himself in 1806. American Express offered to fund conservation of the painting by donating 5 cents to $5 every time someone in the Cincinnati area used an American Express product or service. In addition, the company allocated thousands of dollars usually spent on traditional marketing to promote the fund drive. Newspaper and magazine advertisements explaining the program promoted the museum as well.

For its part, the museum put the cleaning and restoration of the painting on display in a windowed enclosure in one of its galleries, so visitors could watch conservators at work. Labels explained the process and acknowledged the financial support of the people of Cincinnati and American Express. When the painting was rehung in its familiar place, the entire community took pride in the event.

American Express' dynamic fund-raising program has now included projects in 50 U.S. cities, Puerto Rico, Canada and the United Kingdom. A three-month campaign raised $105,000 to help construct a new building and modernize support systems at Mount Vernon, George Washington's home near Alexandria, Virginia. The company also sponsored a national campaign in support of the restoration of the Statue of Liberty. Initially American Express pledged $1 million, but the three-month project raised $1.7 million. The most recent effort was launched on behalf of the Lincoln Park Zoo in Chicago.

For American Express, cause-related marketing is as successful as any of its other marketing programs, and everybody benefits. The company gains customers, cultural institutions raise money, and individuals are offered a simple way to show their support for cultural causes. As one American Express advertisement concludes, "At the same time you're showing yourself a good time, you'll be showing the museum you're behind it all the way. It's an easy way for all of us to say 'Bravo!'"

to go. Though committed to public accessibility, they raise fees for services and admissions.

The economic conditions of the beginning of this decade have forced a fundamental shift in the outlook of museums toward their future financial stability. Times *are* hard, and money for museums *is* scarce. In many parts of the United States economic conditions are not expected to improve substantially in the near future. In truth, the hard facts of diminishing resources are already forcing Americans to revise their expectations about the quality of their lives.

Some observers say economic change need not make matters worse, simply different. Daniel Yankelovich suggests that Americans think not in terms of setbacks or crises but accept economic change as a stimulus for careful examination of values and priorities. In the process, he says, a new range of beneficial choices will likely come into view. By taking action, rather than passively reacting and adjusting to adverse circumstances, the quality of life may well be enhanced.

Museum trustees and directors faced with rising personnel costs, overcrowded storage areas and aging buildings might find it difficult at first to take Yankelovich's suggestion seriously. But if resources are static or diminishing and there is little other recourse that would maintain the level of activity and standards of excellence necessary to fulfill the museum's mission, then looking for opportunity might, in fact, be the best option.

A new approach is needed, for the rapid economic growth we have known in the past is unlikely to return soon to America. The future financial stability of museums will depend on their capacity to address their economic prospects methodically and with an innovative eye. Some museums have already engaged in effective lobbying, aggressive fund raising, improved fiscal management, imaginative efforts to conserve resources and generate earned income and serious reassessments of goals and possibilities. These are signs of a new realism and a fierce survival instinct, and welcome assurance that the uses of adversity, if not sweet, can be productive.

A Special Blend of Financial Support

The museum community can be proud of its system of financial support. Museums are a joint venture. They generate the resources to carry out their work by blending the contributions of individuals, businesses, foundations, and government at the federal, state and local levels. Some of these contributions come in the form of the in-kind donation of equipment or services. Added to the mixture is income generated by the museum's own programs and services, and, for some fortunate institutions, its endowment.

A survey conducted in 1979 by the Institute of Museum Services reveals the mixed system of financial support that distinguishes this country's museums. Of nearly $1 billion in total operating income, 6.9 percent came from the federal government, 12.4 percent from state government and 18.7 percent from local government. Individual contributions, memberships, corporations, foundations and miscellaneous private sources made up 21.3 percent. Admission fees, gift shop sales, restaurant income and the like accounted for 26.5 percent of total income, while revenue from non-operating sources (investments and endowments) amounted to 14.2 percent.

Direct federal funding has enabled museums to mount important exhibitions, engage in significant scholarly activity, provide the public with new kinds of education programs and care more adequately for collections. Still, the percentages show that federal dollars form just a small part of the overall support for museums; their indirect impact is what makes the difference. By requiring that federal dollars be matched with private dollars, the National Endowments for the Arts and the Humanities stimulate private giving to museums. Because of the endowments' grant review panel system, federal support for a project is a peer stamp of approval that in turn guides corporations and foundations in their own grant-making decisions. The NEA and NEH challenge grant programs have stimulated the growth of museum endowments, generated substantial new private support and encouraged museums to institute sound planning practices. National Science Foundation support for innovative education programs has enabled museums to experiment with potentially fruitful new approaches. IMS general operating support grants have had an indirect benefit,

Art in the Marketplace

For centuries the marketplace was a common ground where people gathered to buy and sell, be entertained, hear the latest news and meet friends. The arts always flourished. Artists, musicians, dancers and craftsmen gravitated to the marketplace, which served both material and spiritual needs.

Today's marketplace is the suburban shopping mall. In an attempt to restore the arts to their historic position, the Rouse Company's Art in the Marketplace Program has, since 1977, sponsored art, musical performances, museums and special events in Rouse-built shopping malls. Rouse—a publicly owned real estate, finance, development and management company—designed the program to take advantage of the positive stimulation the arts offer and to help local and national arts organizations and cultural institutions to reach broader audiences.

During Art in the Marketplace's seven years, 13 museums have opened in malls across the country. The Baltimore Museum of Art opened the first in Columbia, Maryland, where the Rouse Company is headquartered. Rouse equipped and furnished the exhibition area, and recently enlarged it. The museum provides eight traveling exhibitions a year, and the mall pays for mounting them. The Franklin Institute Science Museum in Philadelphia offered exhibitions and live science demonstrations at the Science Bar in the Gallery at Market East. The University of Southern California operates the Atelier in Santa Monica Place, a laboratory exhibition gallery for USC's master's degree museum studies program as well as an exhibition space and meeting place for seminars and lectures. And during the extensive renovations of its main building, the Museum of Fine Arts in Boston maintained a branch museum at Faneuil Hall.

The costs associated with branch museums are extensive. While the Rouse Company donates space free of charge and often contributes to the initial exhibit installation, the museum must bear the costs related to staffing and maintaining a mall branch. Some museums like the idea of branches but simply cannot afford them. Most of the successful mall museums have supplemented the Rouse contribution through extensive fund raising. The Science Bar, for example, was made possible through grants from the National Endowment for the Arts, the National Science Foundation and the Fund for the Improvement of Post Secondary Education.

On the other hand, mall branches can help museums build audiences and establish financial stability. The Staten Island Children's Museum, which is in the process of moving from a small storefront location to a larger, permanent site, installed its popular exhibit, *Once upon an Island*, in the busy Staten Island Mall. Fully staffed, the branch features guided tours, workshops and demonstrations about the life of Staten Island's early settlers. More than 50 percent of the visitors have never been to a museum, and the museum staff hopes they will return to the new permanent site.

The South Street Seaport Museum in New York City has a unique partnership with Rouse. To build a solid financial base, the museum invited the company to develop portions of the property it had acquired along the East River. Each contributes to maintenance and security and has the right to review and approve the other's plans.

For Rouse, collaboration with museums is good business. Says founder James W. Rouse, "The computerized, prepackaged, fast-paced world is softened, warmed and slowed down by the presence of the museum, the dancer, the actor—all in the midst of the market. Everyone wins."

too, in stimulating museums to assert the importance of funding for operational expenses.

Corporate support for museums also has an indirect value. Many of the large special exhibitions of the past decade, which generated substantial public interest in museums, drew new audiences and increased museum memberships, would not have been possible without the generosity of corporations. Businesses also make in-kind contributions of equipment and their employees' professional expertise. Often in conjunction with exhibitions, they help museums market their programs and services more effectively and to a wider audience. Corporations such as the Rouse Company, Philip Morris, Inc., and Champion Paper provide space for museums in malls and office buildings; still others have impressive collections of their own and exhibit them to the public. Many museums have formal relationships with business leaders in their communities through special advisory groups or corporate membership programs. Museums are also entering into joint business ventures with corporations—copublishing books and catalogs, marketing lines of products based on a museum's collection, developing computer software.

The importance of such corporate contributions to museum programs with public appeal should not obscure the fact that, with few exceptions, support for operating expenses is not popular with the business community. Businesses are usually motivated to support museums by the visibility they receive in return. If museums are to attract corporate support for operating expenses and other pressing needs that lack an obvious public component, it is up to them to find visible ways to acknowledge this support.

Recent Challenges and Future Prospects

Despite the healthy pluralism of financial support, there have been challenges to the financial health of museums during the past four years. Direct federal funding of museums through the Institute of Museum Services, the National Museum Act, the National Science Foundation and the National Endowments for the Arts and the Humanities has been curtailed or threatened with curtailment. The indirect impact of other federal cutbacks—the Comprehensive Employment and

The Debate over the Charitable Deduction

With the blessing and encouragement of the federal government, American citizens give billions of dollars each year to public charities. Since 1917 the United States Tax Code has contained provisions that stimulate private giving for the public good. For museums, the charitable deduction has been the single most important federal policy affecting their well being. Financial data collected by the Institute of Museum Services in 1979 show that private support constituted 21 percent of the total operating budgets of museums—a figure that excludes the value of the objects and materials donated for collections. Although giving is not prompted solely by tax incentives, there is no denying the cumulative effect of the deduction on the growth and vitality of the nation's museums, their collections and their prospects for long-term financial stability.

Despite abundant evidence that the charitable deduction has worked to the public's benefit in countless areas of our national life, including museums, the deduction and the assumptions upon which it is based are proving vulnerable to the pressures created by large federal deficits, the search for revenue and the move to reduce the complexities and contradictions of the nation's tax system. With only 25 percent of the nation's citizens earning enough to itemize their returns, and therefore take advantage of the full range of deductions, arguments for tax equity strengthen the impetus for reform.

Current proposals to simplify the tax code and redress apparent inequities would eliminate all but a few deductions. Among the half dozen proposals introduced in Congress in 1983 and 1984, only two would provide a deduction for charitable giving. In each case, the tax incentive offered is much smaller than the current incentive, particularly for individuals in the upper income brackets.

For museums, the effect of such a reduction would have serious, long-term consequences on both their financial stability and the growth of their collections. Large voluntary organizations, likeUnited Way, depend on millions of citizens making small donations to support their work, while museums depend on far fewer, and much larger, donations. Most private support for the cultural community comes from individuals with incomes of more than $50,000, for whom the tax advantages of giving are significant.

A system of tax incentives that effectively maintains and increases private support of public charities is essential to the future well being of museums and all those they serve. The AAM's Legislative Program is working to make sure this position is clearly voiced in the debate over the charitable deduction.

Training Act, for example, or cuts to education programs—is more difficult to assess, but still very real.

Cutbacks in federal support have awakened the museum community to the interrelationship among all these sources of funding and, in particular, to the critical position of federal support. Threats to federal funding have a ripple effect on other sources. State legislatures and municipal and county governments follow the federal lead, so the shift in federal attitude toward support of cultural activities makes them an easy target for cuts at other levels of government. The effect of recent federal cutbacks is already evident; the National Assembly of State Arts Agencies says 20 states reported decreases in state funding for the arts in 1983, in contrast to 12 in 1982. Still another manifestation of the reduced federal commitment to cultural, educational and social programs is the increasingly intense competition for the private sector gift. Here museums find themselves pitted against human service and educational organizations and higher education.

The museum community has responded aggressively and effectively to the recent economic adversity. Articulate statements of the case for a federal commitment to museums helped prevent drastic curtailment of federal funds. In fiscal year 1984, for example, funding from the IMS, NEA and NEH—just three of the five major federal agencies that support museums—totaled $41 million, instead of the $24.2 million proposed by the Reagan administration. Still, this amount is only a small fraction of the nearly $1 billion estimated as needed to operate the nation's museums.

Museums have become more effective at managing their resources prudently. Often with the assistance of the private sector, many have sought to improve their management practices. Museums have also been more aggressive about raising funds and increasing earned income. In a Museums Collaborative, Inc., survey, museum directors said they saw significant potential for income from museum shops, restaurants, publications, fees for special programs and other activities. Many museums are allocating more staff time for development; a few have initiated coordinated fund-raising efforts. Other museums are exploring a wide range of creative avenues for increasing income.

Despite the tenacity and ingenuity of museums, their long-term financial stability continues to be of concern. The tenor of national policy still favors a diminished government role. Once again, appropriations requests for fiscal year 1985 propose cuts in funds for the federal agencies that support museums.

The tenor of national policy also favors the stimulation of private initiative, but to date increases in individual or private support of museums have been modest. *Giving USA*, the American Association of Fund-Raising Counsel's compilation of facts and trends in philanthropy, reports that in 1983 private giving to the arts and humanities rose by 11.4 percent over 1982. One factor in the $4.08 billion increase was the creation of the National Arts Stabilization Fund with $9 million from three foundations; the fund will serve primarily the performing arts and art museums. Giving in the arts and the humanities constituted 6.2 percent of all philanthropy, the same as in 1982.

Contributions to museums and historical societies represent just 4.9 percent of total foundation giving, while educational institutions receive about one-third of all foundation dollars awarded. Foundations gave $88.12 million to museums in 1983, almost exactly the same amount as 1982 ($88.17). *Giving USA* reports corporate giving in culture and the arts in 1982 (the latest figures available) increased 4.5 percent from 1981; the $145.8 billion in contributions represented 11.4 percent of all corporate philanthropy, just slightly less than 1981 (11.9 percent).

The previous year, *Giving USA* had concluded that for cultural organizations, there were hard times ahead, but the latest report is more optimistic. AAFRC president John J. Schwartz praises both nonprofit organizations and their supporters for their response to the past decade's economic conditions, but warns that although nonprofits have shown considerable skill at managing resources and raising money, "there is little hope that most charitable organizations will again be able to reach the level of services they provided as recently as 1980."

Elsewhere in this commission report, we have recommended that the museum community build on the sound advocacy skills it has used at the federal level to make a stronger case for museums with leaders in business, foundations and state and local governments. We have applauded the federal lobbying effort, which is really just gaining momentum, as absolutely essential if museums are to be heard when they assert the obligation of government. We have also noted the success of

Minnesota's Keystone Awards Program

The Minneapolis–St. Paul metropolitan area is often cited for its high "quality of life." This is not surprising, since businesses throughout Minnesota take their social responsibility seriously.

The Minnesota Keystone Awards began in 1976 when David Koch, president of Graco, Inc., and then president of the Minneapolis Chamber of Commerce, wanted to make advancing business commitment to social responsibility a major goal of the chamber. At the time businesses were allowed to deduct a maximum of 5 percent of pretax earnings for charitable contributions. Koch knew that Dayton-Hudson, a Minneapolis corporation, had been contributing at the maximum level to social programs and the arts for more than 30 years, and he set out to identify other businesses that were contributing at a similar level. He expected to find eight or 10, but discovered there were 23. That year the Minnesota 5 Percent Investment Program, or the 5 Percent Club, as it is often called, was born.

Chief executive officers from the 23 member corporations were determined to encourage other businesses to examine their giving programs and consider joining the ranks of the 5 percenters. Today 70 Minnesota companies contribute at least 5 percent of their pretax earnings to charitable and community projects. To honor the many businesses not contributing 5 percent but still giving far beyond the national average, the Chamber of Commerce instituted the Minnesota 2 Percent Community Partnership Awards in 1980. These awards recognize the 33 companies that contribute at least double the corporate average of one percent of their pretax earnings.

The third component of the Keystone program—the Creative Community Projects Awards—was also established in 1980. This program recognizes organizations that use company resources to meet community needs "through community programming, lending employees as volunteers, strategic social investments or other programs." Among the programs recognized is B. Dalton's National Literacy Initiative Program, which teaches people to read.

The special relationship between business and the community in Minnesota is a model. The Twin Cities group has received so many inquiries about what makes the relationship work that it has developed a guidebook, *Corporate Social Responsibility: "Minnesota Strategies."* It is available through the Greater Minneapolis Chamber of Commerce.

Collaborative Fund Raising

"Join Alice and step through the looking glass," announces the invitation to the COMPAS Nine black-tie dinner and auction in Phoenix, Arizona. "Alice in Wonderland" was the theme, and Phoenix community leaders seemed like Tweedledum and Tweedledee, who "went off hand-in-hand into the woods, and returned in a minute with their arms full of things." COMPAS—Combined Metropolitan Phoenix Arts and Sciences—is a nonprofit organization dedicated to enhancing the city's cultural environment. Since its inception in 1967, the group has raised more than $2 million for its beneficiaries—the Phoenix Art Museum, the Phoenix Symphony Orchestra, the Heard Museum and the Phoenix Zoo. In turn, the real winners have been the more than 1.4 million people who visited the museums or zoo or attended orchestra performances in these years, and the city of Phoenix itself.

COMPAS raises funds from cash donations and from four auction events held every two years. The process takes considerably longer than it took Tweedledum and Tweedledee; planning for the auctions begins more than a year in advance, and a full-time staff now administers COMPAS operations. But COMPAS volunteers do gather all sorts of wonderful things — a trip for two to Kona, Hawaii; a VIP weekend package for the opening of the Chicago Cubs season; dinner at the home of Erma and Bill Bombeck; and for the recent auction, Salvador Dali's version of *Alice's Adventures in Wonderland*.

COMPAS Nine, held in spring 1983, raised more than $600,000. As with other fund raisers, each beneficiary receives an equal share, and decides independently how the money will be spent. The Phoenix Art Museum, for example, reports that 55 percent of its COMPAS funds are used for exhibitions and 45 percent for the acquisition of new works of art. COMPAS has helped the Heard Museum of Anthropology and Primitive Art, noted for its collection of Southwest Indian arts and crafts, acquire several works of art including a totem sculpture. The museum is also in the midst of a major expansion partially funded with COMPAS money.

COMPAS recently added two more features to its program. In 1982, members of all four COMPAS beneficiaries participated in a "sports in support of culture" golf tournament underwritten by the First Phoenician Corporation. And in recognition of their responsibility to educate tomorrow's cultural patrons, COMPAS beneficiaries have begun a new awareness program aimed at teaching elementary school children what the arts can offer them personally and what arts and cultural organizations do for the general public.

The COMPAS slogan is "The gift that gives in return." The benefits COMPAS brings to the people and cultural community of Phoenix make that more than evident.

museums in generating earned income. And we have urged an aggressive approach to marketing the assets of museums to opinion leaders and the general public, so the private affection people feel for museums becomes a strong base of philosophical support. We are suggesting that ultimately museums must be the guarantors of their own well-being. Sound management is essential in these difficult times, to ensure that every dollar of revenue is well spent. Recognizing that the economic situation of nonprofit institutions is likely to remain uncertain, we suggest that museums collectively and individually use their strong position as respected institutions to strengthen their base of financial support and diversify it further.

In light of what we have learned about the economic condition of American museums today, and in consideration of the societal trends with particular implications for museums, we conclude that the most pressing financial needs of museums now and in the future are for general operating costs and the development of endowments for operating expenses; the care and organization of collections; and capital expenses.

General operating expenses—the simple but staggering daily costs of running a museum—are difficult to fund through public and private resources. The exception is the Institute of Museum Services, which has made general operating support grants since its inception in 1977. Still, IMS appropriations for this purpose in fiscal year 1984 totaled only $15.7 million, a scant proportion of the nearly $1 billion estimated to be the total cost of keeping the doors of this nation's museums open. With basic costs rising and public use of museums increasing, it is imperative that there be a broader commitment to general operating support grants from all sources. Museums should be encouraged to develop and build endowment funds earmarked for museum operations.

Concerning the care and organization of collections, chapter 2 of this report gives ample evidence that museum collections must be the focus of new initiatives. Capital expenses are a further need. Many museums are housed in aging buildings requiring structural repairs and renovation, not to mention their need for additional storage and exhibition space.

We see other financial requirements, too. Increasing recognition of museums as educational institutions indicates that museums merit more support for public programs and activities. Programs, exhibitions or administrative systems planned and carried out in collaboration with other museums or cultural organizations may be possible only through innovative methods of funding. To enable museums to take full advantage of computer technology, money is needed to initiate or improve computerized collections management systems and to use electronic technology in exhibitions and public programs. In-kind contributions of goods and services can be extremely effective in this regard. Just as any new business needs venture capital, museums need the start-up funds for activities that could produce income. Beginning a merchandising program, expanding publishing activity, opening a new restaurant or museum shop—all require an investment most museums are unable to make from their operating budgets. Finally, to stimulate innovation, ensure excellence and offer increased incentives for museum employees, money must be available for higher salaries and continuing professional development in academic disciplines as well as in the fields of education, conservation and audience research. It must also make possible stipends for continuing education in management and grants for individual travel.

◆ RECOMMENDATION 16: Museums should increase their efforts toward achieving a more secure financial base for the future through a combination of sound management, self-help and appeals for public and private support. The benefits museums bring to a community and the nation must be demonstrated, and government officials must be more aware of their responsibility in the partnership of financial support. In particular, the necessity for federal leadership in commitment to museums as irreplaceable national resources must be aggressively and persistently emphasized. To generate a more balanced support for all facets of museum programs and operations, the museum community must explain its needs to government officials at all levels and to leaders in corporations and foundations. At the same time, museums should vigorously pursue cost-saving opportunities and creative ventures to increase earned income. They must continue to strive for the best in management practices.

Notes and Sources

Chapter 1

Page 17: Kevin Starr, a columnist for the *San Francisco Examiner*, referred to Aristotle during the commission's San Francisco open forum, November 15–16, 1982.

Page 17: The most recent comprehensive survey of United States museums was published in 1979 by the National Center for Education Statistics for the Institute of Museum Services, Washington, D.C. The *Museum Universe Survey* estimated the number of museums in the United States at nearly 5,000, including art, history and science museums, historic houses, science-technology centers, aquariums, botanical gardens, arboretums, nature centers, zoos, children's museums, park museums and visitor centers. For more information about the survey, see "American Museums: The Vital Statistics," by Lee Kimche, former director of the IMS, in *Museum News*, October 1980, p. 52.

Page 18: Alan Jacobs, chairman of the Department of City and Regional Planning, University of California, Berkeley, and Kevin Starr, columnist for the *San Francisco Examiner*, made these observations about museums at the San Francisco open forum.

Page 18: Nathaniel Burt describes the evolution of the American museum in *Palaces for the People: A Social History of the American Art Museum* (Boston: Little, Brown and Company, 1977), p. 14.

Page 18: Benjamin Ives Gilman, secretary of the Museum of Fine Arts, Boston, wrote about the educational aims of museums in *Museum Ideals of Purpose and Method* (Cambridge, Mass.: Harvard University Press, 1923).

Page 19: Stephen Weil, deputy director of the Hirshhorn Museum and Sculpture Garden, Smithsonian Institution, describes the relationship of museums to society in "No Museum Is an Island," *Museum News*, January/February 1981, pp. 67, 80–88. The essay is included in Weil's *Beauty and the Beasts: On Museums, Art, the Law, and the Market* (Washington, D.C.: Smithsonian Institution Press, 1983).

Page 20: The first report on the economic impact of museums was the National Endowment for the Arts,

Economic Impact of Arts and Cultural Institutions, Research Division Report 15 (New York: Publishing Center for Cultural Resources, 1981). Economic information about New England museums is available from the New England Foundation for the Arts, 25 Mount Auburn St., Cambridge, Mass. 02138. Information presented here is from *The Arts and the New England Economy*, 2d ed. (Cambridge, Mass.: New England Foundation for the Arts, 1981).

The economic impact of the Portland Museum of Art is described in an article by Nancy Love in the *Wall Street Journal*, October 26, 1983, p.26.

Study findings about the attractiveness of cities for prospective businesses are based on responses from a probability sample of 1,290 firms in 10 central cities—Atlanta, Dallas, Detroit, Los Angeles, Minneapolis, New York, Phoenix, Pittsburgh, Seattle and St. Louis. Findings are published in "Central City Business: Plans and Problems," a study prepared for the Subcommittee on Fiscal and Intergovernmental Policy, Joint Economic Committee of the U.S. Congress, January 1979.

Page 21: For more information about the resources available to small history museums, write the American Association for State and Local History, 126 Second Ave., N., Nashville, Tenn. 37201.

Page 22: The conditions that will shape the 21st century are described by Asa Briggs in "Looking Back from the Twenty-First Century," an essay included in *Communications in the Twenty-First Century*, ed. Robert W. Haigh, George Gerbner and Richard B. Byrne (New York: John Wiley & Sons, 1981). Briggs is provost of Worcester College, Oxford, and chancellor of the Open University.

Page 22: Peter H. Raven, director of the Missouri Botanical Garden, summarizes trends in world population growth in "Knockdown-Dragout on the Global Future," a paper presented to the American Association for the Advancement of Science at its conference on "Global Future: The Third World," held in May 1984 in New York City.

Page 23: In identifying the forces of change that are important to museums, the commission found the following useful: Marilyn Ferguson, *The Aquarian Conspiracy: Personal and Social Transformation in the 1980s* (Los Angeles: J. P. Tarcher, 1980); Joel Garreau, *The Nine Nations of North America* (Boston: Houghton Mifflin, 1981); Landon Y. Jones, *Great Expectations: America and the Baby Boom Generation* (New York: Coward, McCann and Geoghegan, 1980); John Naisbitt, *Megatrends* (New York: Warner, 1982); David Pearce Snyder, "The Information Age: Rationalized Life Styles," in *The Future of Vocational Education*, ed. Gordon I. Swanson (Arlington, Va.: American Vocational Association, 1981), pp. 123–50; and Daniel Yankelovich, *New Rules* (New York: Random House, 1981).

More specific information about museums and the future was the topic of "Looking Ahead: Identifying the Shape of the Future," a report prepared in spring 1982 by Gail Anderson, an intern for the commission, now assistant director of programs and development at the Southwest Museum in Los Angeles.

Page 24: Population data are from reports of the U.S. Census Bureau, Washington, D.C., and the Population Reference Center, Washington, D.C. Reports from the Trend Analysis Program of the American Council of Life Insurance are the source of information about the changing nature of work, technology, life extension, institutions in an information era and cultural pluralism. Representatives from the Values and Lifestyles Program of SRI International in Menlo Park, California; the Naisbitt Group in Washington, D.C., and Los Angeles, California; and Yankelovich, Skelly and White in New York City provided the commission with information and insights on changing attitudes and values among Americans. Other information was obtained from the staff, members and publications of the World Future Society in Washington, D.C., the Congressional Research Service of the Library of Congress and the House Committee on Science and Technology of the U.S. Congress.

Page 25: The commission studied three recent reports on American education: Ernest Boyer, for the Carnegie Foundation for the Advancement of Teaching, *High School: A Report on Secondary Education in America* (New York: Harper & Row, 1983); National Commission on Excellence in Education, *A Nation at Risk: The Imperative for Educational Reform* (Washington, D.C.: U.S. Government Printing Office, 1983); and National Science Board Commission on Precollege Education in Mathematics, Science and Technology, *Educating Americans for the 21st Century* (Washington, D.C.: National Science Foundation, 1983).

Page 28: Population figures for Florida, Texas and California are from the U.S. Census Bureau, Washington D.C. The western states with a total of 30 new art museums include Arizona, California, New Mexico, Oregon, Texas and Washington. Figures on growth of museums are from the California Arts Council, the Florida Division of Cultural Affairs and the Texas As-

sociation of Museums. Information about the attitudes of adults toward the arts is from National Research Center for the Arts, *Americans and the Arts* (New York: American Council for the Arts, 1981).

Chapter 2

Page 36: General statistics about objects in museum collections are based on information the commission received from individual museums and museum associations. Stephen Edwards, executive director of the Association of Systematics Collections at the University of Kansas in Lawrence, provided data about existing biological collections and projections for the future.

Page 36: The information about collections growth at the San Diego Museum of Man, Munson-Williams-Proctor Institute, McKinley Museum of History, Science and Industry, Albright-Knox Art Gallery, Southeast Arkansas Arts and Science Center and the Florida State Museum came from the commission's National Monitoring System. A pilot research project established by the commission to acquire information about trends in museums, the monitoring system involved 62 museums selected through a stratified random sampling procedure. Data were collected with the assistance of a monitor in each museum who gathered information and communicated it in telephone conversations or by mail to an interviewer at the commission office. Anecdotal material drawn from monitoring system communications appears throughout this report.

Page 36: *Museum Ethics*, published by the American Association of Museums (Washington, D.C., 1978) is the AAM's official statement on the ethical principles underlying all areas of museum operations.

Page 37: For further reading on collecting contemporary material, see Robert Asher, "How to Build a Time Capsule," *Journal of Popular Culture*, Fall 1974, pp. 241–53; Sigfried Giedion, *Mechanization Takes Command: A Contribution to Anonymous History* (New York: W. W. Norton, 1948); Chester H. Liebs, "Remember Our Not-So-Distant Past?" *Historic Preservation*, January/March 1978, pp. 30–35; Edith Mayo, "Connoisseurship of the Future," in *Twentieth-Century Popular Culture in Museums and Libraries*, ed. F. E. H. Schroeder (Bowling Green, Ohio: Bowling Green University Popular Press, 1981); Marshall McLuhan, *Understanding Media* (New York: Signet Books, 1966); David Orr and Mark Ohno, "The Material Culture of Protest: A Case Study in Contemporary Collecting," in *Twentieth-Century Popular Culture in Museums and Libraries*, pp. 37–54; William Rathje, "The Garbage Project: A New Way to Look at the Problems of Archaeology," *Archaeology*, October 1974, pp. 236–41; Barbara Riley, "Contemporary Collecting: A Case Study," *Decorative Arts Newsletter*, Summer 1978, pp. 3–6; Goran Rosander, *Today for Tomorrow: Museum Documentation of Contemporary Society in Sweden by Acquisition of Objects* (Stockholm: SAMDOK Council, 1980); Mark Schiffer and Richard Gould, *Modern Material Culture: The Archaeology of Us* (New York: Academic Press, 1981); Thomas J. Schlereth, "Collecting Today for Tomorrow," *Museum News*, March/April 1982, pp. 29–37; Robert Venturi, et al., *Learning from Las Vegas* (Cambridge, Mass.: MIT Press, 1972).

Page 37: See Maria Papageorge, "Collecting the Present in Sweden," *Museum News*, September/October 1981, pp. 13ff. For more information about SAMDOK or for a copy of the report, *Today for Tomorrow*, write to Gunilla Cedrenius, SAMDOK Secretariat, Nordiska Museet, S-115 21 Stockholm, Sweden.

Page 38: The figures about dangers of extinction are from the American Association of Zoological Parks and Aquariums. A brochure about the Species Survival Plan is available from AAZPA, Oglebay Park, Wheeling, West Virginia 26003.

Page 40: The David Hugh Smith quotation is from an article in the *Christian Science Monitor*, May 3, 1982.

Page 40: Marie C. Malaro's "Collections Management Policies," *Museum News*, November/December 1979, pp. 57–61, is a good guide to collections management.

General references concerning collections care, maintenance and conservation include these publications of the National Institute for the Conservation of Cultural Property, Arts and Industries Building, Room 2225, Smithsonian Institution,Washington, D.C. 20560: *Conservation of Cultural Property in the United States* (1976); *Conservation Treatment Facilities in the United States* (1980); *Report of the Study Committee on Education and Training* (1979); *Report of the Study Committee on Libraries and Archives* (1978); *Report of the Study Committee on Scientific Support* (1979); *Suggested Guidelines for Training in Architectural Conservation* (1980).

The American Association of Museums publishes *Museum News* reprints on the care of collections, including conservation, collections management policies and storage. *Museum Registration Methods* (Washington, D.C.: American Association of Museums, 1979) describes standard procedures for recording information about objects. The AAM publications office is located at 1055 Thomas Jefferson St., NW, Washington, D.C. 20007.

The American Association for State and Local History's *Bibliography on Historical Organization Practices*, ed. Frederick L. Rath, Jr., and Merrilyn Rogers O'Connell, is a six-volume reference work that provides sources of information to guide all areas of historical agency administration, including *Historic Preservation* (vol. 1); *Care and Conservation of Collections* (vol. 2); *Interpretation* (vol. 3); *Documentation of Collections* (vol. 4); *Administration* (vol. 5); *Research* (vol. 6). The AASLH address is given in the note for page 21.

Page 41: The American Institute for Conservation (AIC) is a professional organization for individuals trained in the conservation of cultural materials. Members must meet minimum professional requirements for acceptance and subscribe to the institute's code of ethics and standards of practice. AIC has worked to increase both the public's and the museum community's understanding of conservation as a scientific process. It has improved treatment of objects by fostering scientific research and has protected objects and materials from inappropriate and damaging treatment. Its meetings and publications enable conservators to learn about new techniques and to explore ethical issues that surround the process of conserving and preserving cultural materials. AIC's address is 3545 Williamsburg Lane, NW, Washington, D.C. 20008.

The National Institute for the Conservation of Cultural Property (NIC) was established in 1982, replacing the National Conservation Advisory Council (NCAC). As a national forum and clearinghouse for information on conservation, NIC has a membership that includes institutions only—conservation training and education programs, institutions with conservation treatment or research facilities, area conservation membership organizations. As NCAC, the institute published studies focusing on major concerns in a variety of disciplines. NIC's address is given above.

Page 41: For further information on the statewide inventory in Indiana, contact Nikki Black, Children's Museum, P.O. Box 3000, Indianapolis, Ind. 46206. Write Laura Sprague, 28 Orchard St., Portland, Maine 04102, for more information about Maine's inventory project.

Page 42: *America's Museums: The Belmont Report*, a precedent for this commission, was published in 1969 by the American Association of Museums.

Page 42: Observations about the state of conservation come from *Conservation Treatment Facilities in the United States* (Washington, D.C.: National Conservation Advisory Council, 1980).

Page 42: *Museums USA*, published by the NEA (Washington, D.C., 1974) was the first publication to present a comprehensive picture of museums—including numbers and locations, types and functions, facilities and finances, personnel and trustees, activities and attendance. Research for *Museums USA* was conducted by the National Research Center of the Arts, an affiliate of Louis Harris and Associates; statistics on page 183.

Page 42: In fiscal year 1984, Congress approved funds for the Institute of Museum Services to initiate a new program of grants for conservation and related activities. Congress also requested that the American Association of Museums, in cooperation with the National Institute for Conservation and the American Institute for Conservation, study the current state of the nation's collections, the conservation needs in museums of all kinds and the adequacy of conservation training, personnel and services to meet those needs. Surveys of the museum community and the conservation field will result in quantitative data on all types of museums. Related research projects will look at public and private support for collections-related activities, public programming in conservation subjects and the availability of conservation training for museum professionals other than conservators. The results of the study will be available through the AAM late in 1984.

With a grant from the National Endowment for the Humanities, the AAM organized five colloquiums on the care of collections essential to the humanities. Problems of art, history and anthropology/archeology collections and developments in conservation, maintenance and documentation were discussed by a cross-section of museum personnel, conservators and scholars. A report summarizing the findings of the colloquiums, including recommendations and priorities, will also be available through the AAM in the fall of 1984.

Page 42: Philippe de Montebello, director of the Metropolitan Museum of Art, describes how financial constraints and the need to generate revenue through popular exhibits are altering the character and traditional values of museums in "The High Cost of Quality," *Museum News*, August 1984, pp. 47–49; quotation from p. 47.

Page 42: The statistics about directors' priorities for the museum's function and purpose are from *Museums USA*, p. 25; budgetary priorities are from p. 181.

Page 43: Information about National Endowment for the Arts grants to museums is from the endowment's annual reports, 1971–82. For general information about the Museum Program, see *Guide to the National Endowment for the Arts*; for specific grant information, see *Application Guidelines*. NEA annual reports, program guidelines and application guidelines are available through the NEA, Museum Program, 1100 Pennsylvania Ave., NW, Washington, D.C. 20506.

For information about National Museum Act grants, see *National Museum Act Guidelines: Grant Programs for Professional Training and Assistance in Conservation and Museum Practices*, available from National Museum Act, Arts and Industries Building, Smithsonian Institution, Washington, D.C. 20560.

The Institute of Museum Services publishes yearly editions of *General Operating Support Grant Application and Information*. For a copy, write IMS, 1100 Pennsylvania Ave., NW, Washington, D.C. 20506.

Museum grants from the National Endowment for the Humanities are described in *Guidelines and Application Instructions: Humanities Projects in Museums and Historical Organizations*, available through the NEH, Museums and Historical Organizations Program, 1100 Pennsylvania Ave., NW, Washington, D.C. 20506.

The National Science Foundation grant information is from selected program reports available at the foundation, 1800 G St., NW, Washington, D.C. 20550.

Page 46: For general resource information on museums and computers, see *Museum Collections and Computers*, a report of an Association of Systematics Collections Survey, compiled by Lenore Sarasan and A. M. Neuner (Lawrence, Kans.: Association of Systematics Collections, 1983); and Robert G. Chenhall, *Mu-

seum Cataloging in the Computer Age* (Nashville, Tenn.: American Association for State and Local History, 1975).

Page 47: For more information about the Museum Computer Network, write to David Vance, President, Museum Computer Network, Inc., E.C.C., Bldg. 26, State University of New York at Stony Brook, Stony Brook, N.Y. 11794.

For more about the Information Technology Resource Center, write its program director, Steve Andrews, Museum of Science and Industry, 57th St. and Lake Shore Dr., Chicago, Ill. 60637.

The Art Museum Association of America surveyed computer use in *Technology in Museum Environments: A National Survey of Current and Anticipated Computer Use in Art Museums* (San Francisco, 1982).

The information from the Print Council appeared in Marilyn Symmes, "1983 Print Council Survey of the Status of Computerization of Art Collection Information in Museums," an article in the council's 1983 newsletter.

Page 47: ARTIS will be available for purchase by museums in 1985. For further information, contact the Art Museum Association of America, 270 Sutter St., San Francisco, Calif. 94108

Page 48: For an up-to-date discussion of research in museums, see *Museum News*, October 1983. Museum publications reporting on research by museum scholars include, among others, those published by the American Museum of Natural History in New York City, the Field Museum of Natural History in Chicago, the National Gallery of Art's Center for Advanced Study in the Visual Arts in Washington, D.C., and the Henry Francis du Pont Winterthur Museum in Winterthur, Delaware. Conservation research in museums is reported in *Technology and Conservation*.

Page 52: Figures about number of clients and workloads at cooperative conservation centers are from the "Report to the Andrew W. Mellon Foundation on a Grant to Support a Meeting of Regional Conservation Centers," prepared by Arne Hansen, June 1982. Additional information about the Association of Cooperative Conservation Centers can be obtained from Hansen, Rocky Mountain Regional Conservation Center, University of Denver, Denver, Colo. 80208.

Chapter 3

Page 55: The Thomas Jefferson quotation is from "To George Wythe," in *Crusade against Ignorance: Thomas Jefferson on Education*, ed. Gordon C. Lee (New York: Teachers College Press, 1961), pp. 99–100.

Page 55: Among the writings of Benjamin Ives Gilman, Henry Watson Kent and John Cotton Dana about museum education, the following are now considered classics in museum history. John Cotton Dana, *The Gloom of the Museum* (Woodstock, Vt.: Elm Tree Press, 1917),

The New Museum (Woodstock, Vt.: Elm Tree Press, 1917), *A Plan for a New Museum* (Woodstock, Vt.: Elm Tree Press, 1920); Benjamin Ives Gilman, *Museum Ideals of Purpose and Method* (Cambridge, Mass.: Riverside Press, 1918); Henry Watson Kent, *What I Am Pleased to Call My Education* (New York: Grolier Club, 1949). See also Theodore L. Low, *The Educational Philosophy and Practice of Art Museums in the U.S.* (New York: Teachers College, Columbia University, 1948), and *The Museum as a Social Instrument* (New York: Metropolitan Museum of Art for the American Association of Museums, 1942). For a profile of John Cotton Dana, see Richard Grove, "Pioneers in American Museums: John Cotton Dana," *Museum News*, May/June 1978, pp. 32–39, 86–88.

Page 56: Joel N. Bloom's observations on museum outreach are from "A Fresh Look at Creativity," *Museum Magazine*, May/June, 1981, pp. 12ff; quotation from p. 14.

Page 57: The shared purposes of cultural and educational institutions are described by Willard L. Boyd, president of the Field Museum of Natural History in Chicago, in "Linking Cultural and Educational Institutions," *Executive Review*, December 1982, p. 1.

Page 57: Frank Oppenheimer, director of the Exploratorium in San Francisco, spoke about museum learning and museums as places of ideas as the recipient of the American Association of Museums' Distinguished Service to Museums Award in June 1982. His remarks were published in "Exploration and Culture: Oppenheimer Receives Distinguished Service Award," *Museum News*, November/December 1982, pp. 36–45; quotation from p. 39.

Page 57: *Museums: Their New Audiences* (1972) was published by the American Association of Museums.

Page 58: Gary Esolen, editor and publisher of *Gambit*, a New Orleans weekly newspaper, made these remarks during the commission's New Orleans open forum, April 24, 1982. His comments were published in "Dialectic for the Muses," *Museum News*, September/October 1982, pp. 29–31; quotation from p. 31.

Page 59: The information about museum learning and the potential to build cultural self-confidence comes from a paper presented by Nelson H. H. Graburn at the 1982 AAM annual meeting in Philadelphia. Graburn is professor of anthropology at the University of California, Berkeley.

Page 59: Joshua Taylor is quoted in S. Dillon Ripley, "Joshua Taylor: A Museum Is a Bridge That Should Be Well-Traveled," *Art News*, Summer 1981, p. 119.

Page 59: Michael Spock, director of the Children's Museum in Boston, describes "landmark learning" in Enid and Tom Farmer, "A Boston Museum Where Children Can Cavort at Will," *Smithsonian*, October 1981, pp. 158–162ff; quotation from p. 164.

Page 59: Graburn's ideas about museum experiences are described in "The Museum and the Visitor Experience," in *The Visitor and the Museum*, ed. Linda Draper (American Association of Museums, Education Committee, 1977).

Page 63: Neil Harris, professor of history at the University of Chicago, describes the responsibility of museums to offer the visitor a chance to react subjectively to exhibitions in "A Historical Perspective on Museum Advocacy," *Museum News*, November/December 1980, pp. 61–63ff; quotation from p. 86. The article was based on Harris' keynote address during the 1980 AAM annual meeting in Boston.

Page 65: Some sample museum evaluation research reports include Marguerite Bloomberg, *An Experiment in Museum Instruction* (Washington, D.C.: American Association of Museums, 1929); Minda Borun, *Measuring the Immeasurable: A Pilot Study of Museum Effectiveness* (Washington, D.C.: Association of Science-Technology Centers, 1977); Ross Loomis, *Learning about the Denver Art Museum Audience: A Survey of Surveys* (Denver, Colo.: Denver Art Museum, 1983); Mary Ellen Munley, *Evaluation Study Report: Buyin' Freedom, A Dramatic Presentation in the Museum* (Washington, D.C.: Smithsonian Institution, Department of Social and Cultural History, National Museum of American History, 1982); Chandler G. Screven, *The Measurement and Facilitation of Learning in the Museum Environment: An Experimental Analysis* (Washington, D.C.: Smithsonian Institution, Office of Museum Programs, 1974); and Robert L. Wolf and Barbara Tymitz, *"When Will the Fourth Floor Be Open?": A Study of Visitor Perception of the Hirshhorn Museum and Sculpture Garden* (Washington, D.C.: Smithsonian Institution, 1980).

Page 67: The Commission on the Humanities, sponsored by the Rockefeller Foundation, assesses the state of the humanities and points to the special capacities of museums and libraries for learning in *The Humanities in American Life* (Berkeley: University of California Press, 1980), p. 42.

Page 67: Martin Deeks' "Museum-School Collaboration: An Evaluative Study of the Museums Affiliated with Public Schools Program in San Francisco," was completed as a master's thesis for John F. Kennedy University, San Francisco, Calif.

Page 67: Recent commission reports with recommendations concerning museums include the Commission on the Humanities, *The Humanities in American Life*, and the National Science Board Commission on Precollege Education in Mathematics, Science and Technology, *Educating Americans for the 21st Century*.

Page 69: David H. Katzive's observations are from "Museums on the Air," *Museum News*, June 1984, pp. 17–18 ff.

Page 70: Malcolm S. Knowles describes "androgogy" in "The Future of Lifelong Learning," *Museums, Adults and the Humanities*, ed. Zipporah W. Collins (Washington, D.C.: American Association of Museums, 1981), pp. 131–43.

Page 70: For more information about HISTOP, write for a copy of *The HISTOP Handbook* to HISTOP, 1910 Torquay, Royal Oaks, Michigan 48073. Data about the growth of education programming in museums can be found in *Museums USA*.

Page 70: Warren Weaver, Jr., "Smithsonian Flourishes On and Off Its 'Campus,'" *New York Times*, February 8, 1982.

Chapter 4

Page 73: Chester Barnard is quoted in Thomas J. Peters and Robert H. Waterman, Jr., *In Search of Excellence* (New York: Harper & Row, 1982), p. 6.

Page 74: The African-American Museums Association is located at 420 7th St., NW, Washington, D.C. 20004. Other professional associations direct their efforts toward meeting the needs of specialized museums. The largest of these is the American Association for State and Local History in Nashville, Tenn., which serves history museums, historical societies and historic properties. The Association of Science-Technology Centers in Washington, D.C., addresses the interests of this special kind of museum. Though not an official association, the Native American Museums Program, located in the Office of Museum Programs at the Smithsonian Institution, assists those who wish to establish and operate Native American museums. Other specialized associations include the American Association of Botanical Gardens and Arboreta, New Mexico State University, Las Cruces, N. Mex.; American Association of Youth Museums, Los Angeles, Calif.; Association for Living Historical Farms and Agricultural Museums, Augusta, Maine; Association for Railway Museums, Portland, Maine; and the Council of American Maritime Museums, Newport News, Va.

Page 74: The definition of a museum is from the handbook, *Professional Standards for Museum Accreditation*, H. J. Swinney, ed. (Washington, D.C.: American Association of Museums, 1978), p. 9.

In addition to the accreditation handbook, the profession has set down its broad statement of ethical standards in *Museum Ethics*. Guidelines for trustees are found in Alan D. Ullberg with Patricia Ullberg, *Museum Trusteeship* (Washington, D.C.: American Association of Museums, 1981); and Helmuth J. Naumer, *Of Mutual Respect and Other Things: An Essay on Museum Trusteeship* (Washington, D.C.: American Association of Museums, 1977).

Codes of ethics for other museum professionals have also been published. For curators, "A Code of Ethics for Curators," *Museum News*, February 1983, pp. 36–40; for museum stores, "A Code of Ethics for Museum Stores," *Museum News*, January/February 1982, pp. 50–52; for conservators, "A Code of Ethics for Conservators," *Museum News*, March/April 1980, pp. 28–34; for museum training programs and internships, "Criteria for Examining Professional Museum Studies Programs," *Museum News*, June 1983, pp. 70–71, 99–108; for public relations officers, "A Code of Ethics for Public Relations," *Museum News*, October 1984, in press. A code of ethics for registrars will be published by *Museum News* in 1985.

Page 75: Counseling about the accreditation process and additional information about the program are available from the Accreditation Secretary at the American Association of Museums. Information about the accreditation of zoos can be obtained from the American Association of Zoological Parks and Aquariums.

Page 76: William Ruder commented on the role of museums in "Museum Audiences—Bigger Than Ever! But How Big Can We Really Build Them?" a speech he gave at the AAM trustee conference October 9, 1976, in Boston.

Page 76: Thomas M. Messer is quoted in Phillip M. Kadis, "Who Should Manage Museums," *Art News*, October 1977, p. 46.

Page 77: Among the organizations doing research into and acting on behalf of nonprofit institutions are Independent Sector, 1828 L St., NW, Washington, D.C. 20036; Institution for Social and Policy Studies, Yale University, 16A Yale Station, 111 Prospect St., New Haven, Conn. 06520; Association of Governing Boards of Universities and Colleges, 1 Dupont Circle, NW, Washington, D.C. 20036.

Page 78: The Ullberg quotations are from *Museum Trusteeship*, p. 3.

Page 78: Israel Unterman and Richard Hart Davis' article about their study, "The Strategy Gap in Not-for-Profits," was reprinted in *Museum News*, June 1984, pp. 39–44. It was originally published in the *Harvard Business Review*, May/June 1982, pp. 30–40.

Page 78: Edward M. Warburg's remarks were made at a symposium called "Who Runs Museums?" sponsored by Arttable, Inc., in New York. He was quoted in *Art-Wire*, Spring 1984.

Page 79: Information about volunteers is from *American Volunteers—1981*, a Gallup survey on volunteering commissioned by and available from Independent Sector.

Page 81: Dennis Young's working paper, *Incentives and the Nonprofit Sector* (1982), is part of a series on nonprofit management published by Yale's Institution for Social and Policy Studies.

Page 81: Although nationwide salary data for museums are not available, there have been attempts to compile information by discipline and region. The Association of Science-Technology Centers, the Association of Art Museum Directors and the American Association for State and Local History all conduct and publish regularly updated salary surveys. At the state and regional levels, the Texas Association of Museums and the New England Museums Association have both sponsored salary surveys.

Page 83: The information about women in the work force was obtained from the Office of Women, American Council on Education, 1 Dupont Circle, #800, Washington, D.C. 20036; and the Women's College Coalition, 1725 K St., NW, #1003, Washington, D.C. 20036.

Page 83: For more information about the Smithsonian's Career Awareness Program, contact the Office of Elementary and Secondary Education, Arts and Industries Building, Smithsonian Institution, Washington, D.C. 20560. Another career program of interest is Mathematics, Engineering, Science Achievement (MESA), a minority engineering program run by the Lawrence Hall of Science, University of California, Berkeley, Calif. 94720.

Page 85: The Museum Assessment Program (MAP) is a general consultation service designed and conducted by the American Association of Museums to help museums improve the quality of their operations and programs. Since its establishment in 1980, MAP has benefited museums of all kinds and sizes across the nation. For more information about the Museum Assessment Program write to the MAP office at the American Association of Museums.

Page 85: The Regional Conference of Historical Agencies is located at 314 E. Seneca St., Manlius, N.Y. 13104.

Page 86: The *Directory of Louisiana Museums and Exhibition Spaces* is available from the Louisiana Association of Museums, P.O. Box 3373, Baton Rouge, La. 70821. The association will also provide information about its statewide research project.

Chapter 5

Page 89: The Dupont–Kalorama Museums Consortium, 1600 21st St., NW, Washington, D.C. 20009, includes the Phillips Collection, the Textile Museum, the Woodrow Wilson House, the Anderson House, the Columbia Historical Society, the Barney Studio House and the Fondo Del Sol Visual Art and Media Center.

The Science Museum Exhibit Collaborative includes the California Museum of Science and Industry, Los Angeles; the Center of Science and Industry, Columbus, Ohio; the Fort Worth Museum of Science and History; the Franklin Institute Science Museum, Philadelphia; the Museum of Science, Boston; the Museum of Science and Industry, Chicago; the Science Museum of Charlotte, North Carolina; and the Science Museum of Minnesota, St. Paul. The collaborative is headquartered in Boston, with Roger L. Nichols, director of the Museum of Science, serving as secretary/treasurer.

The San Antonio Museum Association includes the San Antonio Museum of Art, the Witte Memorial Museum and the San Antonio Museum of Transportation.

Page 89: Gordon Ambach spoke about networks in a panel discussion at the 1980 AAM annual meeting in Boston. His remarks were published in "Why Museums Need Networks," *Museum News*, November/December 1980, pp.13–17; quotation from p. 14.

Page 91: For information about applying for the international partnerships program, contact the AAM/ICOM Office at the American Association of Museums.

Page 92: For more information about HERPlab, write to HERPlab, Reptile House, National Zoological Park, 3001 Connecticut Ave., NW, Washington, D.C. 20008.

The Gravity Well Exhibit Consortium includes the Milwaukee Public Museum; the Bar Harbor Science Museum, Maine; Discovery Center, Syracuse, N.Y.; Exploreum, Mobile, Ala.; Franklin Institute Science Museum, Philadelphia; Miami Science Center; Milwaukee Museum of Science and Technology; and the Museum of Scientific Discovery, Harrisburg, Pa. For more information, write to Roger Smith, Director, Museum of Scientific Discovery, P.O. Box 934, Strawberry Square, Harrisburg, Pa. 17108.

Page 92: Essays about the collaborative spirit among museum educators are included in *Museums, Adults and the Humanities*. Descriptions of collaborative educational programs undertaken by museums are exemplified in *The Art Museum as Educator*, eds. Barbara Y. Newsom and Adele Z. Silver (Berkeley: University of California Press, 1978); and *Museums, Magic and Children*, ed. Bonnie Pitman-Gelles (Washington, D.C.: Association of Science-Technology Centers, 1981).

Page 93: The Washington State Print Consortium includes the Cheney Cowles Memorial Museum, Spokane; Eastern Washington State Historical Society; Henry Art Gallery, Seattle; Museum of Art, Washington State University, Pullman; Seattle Art Museum; Takoma Art Museum; and the Whatcom Museum of History and Art, Bellingham.

Page 93: For more information about Museum Mile, write to Public Affairs, Museum of the City of New York, Fifth Ave. at 103d St., New York, N.Y. 10029.

Page 94: Waldemar Nielsen's essay, "The Third Sector: Keystone of a Caring Society" appears in *America's Voluntary Spirit*, ed. Brian O'Connell (Washington, D.C.: Foundation Center, 1983) pp. 363–69.

Page 94: The Exploratorium Dissemination Program is one of three projects funded by the Kellogg Foundation. For more about them and information on how to participate, write in care of the Kellogg Project to the Exploratorium, 3601 Lyon St., San Francisco, Calif. 94123; Field Museum of Natural History, Roosevelt Rd. at Lake Shore Dr., Chicago, Ill. 60605; or Office of Museum Programs, Smithsonian Institution, Arts and Industries Building, Washington, D.C. 20560.

Chapter 6

Page 99: Edgar Preston Richardson describes the need for more public awareness about what museums have to offer in "The Core of Our Responsibility," *Museum News*, November/December 1981, pp. 58–60; quotation from p. 59.

Page 103: The Texas Arts Alliance is located at P.O. Box 5513, Austin, Tex. 78763.·

Page 104: Information and samples of the ALA's promotional materials are available from the Public Information Office, American Library Association, 50 E. Huron St., Chicago, Ill. 60611.

Page 106: Marilyn Hood describes the audience evaluation study performed for the Toledo Museum of Art in "Staying Away: Why People Choose Not To Visit Museums," *Museum News*, April 1983, pp. 50–57.

Chapter 7

Page 109: Ralph Waldo Emerson's comment about hard times and the scarcity of money is from the "Works and Days" section of his philosophical essay "Society and Solitude" (1870).

Page 110: Several museums have benefited from American Express' cause-related marketing program. They include the Museum of Contemporary Art in Los Angeles, the San Antonio Museum of Art and the Center of Science and Industry in Des Moines. For more information about the program, contact American Express Company, Corporate Affairs and Communications, American Express Plaza, New York, N.Y. 10004.

Page 110: Daniel Yankelovich describes shifts in American values and their impact on the future in *New Rules* (New York: Random House, 1981).

Page 111: For examples of how selected museums survive reduced government support see Migs Grove, Sybil Walker and Alexandra Walsh, "The Uses of Adversity," *Museum News*, February 1983, pp. 26–35.

Page 111: The information about the percentages of support for museums is based on an analysis by the American Association of Museums' Legislative Program staff of an unpublished Institute of Museum Services survey (1979).

Page 111: More information about federal funding for museums can be obtained from: Institute of Museum Services (IMS), 1100 Pennsylvania Ave., NW, Washington, D.C. 20506, (202) 786-0536 (*Application Guidelines*); National Endowment for the Arts (NEA), 1100 Pennsylvania Ave., NW, Washington, D.C. 20506, (202) 682-2000 (*Annual Report, Guide to the National Endowment for the Arts, Application Guidelines*); National Endowment for the Humanities (NEH), 1100 Pennsylvania Ave., NW, Washington, D.C. 20506, (202) 786-0438 (*Annual Report, Guidelines and Application Instructions: Humanities Projects in Museums and Historical Organizations*); National Historical Publications and Records Commission (NHPRC), National Archives Building, Washington, D.C. 20408, (202) 724-1083; National Museum Act (NMA), Arts and Industries Building, Smithsonian Institution, Washington, D.C. 20506, (202) 357-2257 (*National Museum Act Guidelines: Grant Programs for Professional Training and Assistance in Conservation and Museum*

Practices); National Science Foundation (NSF), Public Information Office, 1800 G St., NW, Washington, D.C. 20550, (202) 357-9498 (*Informal Education Program Guidelines, Annual Report*).

Page 112: A brochure about the Art in the Marketplace Program is available from the Rouse Company, Columbia, Md. 21044.

Page 114: Information on the percentage of the total operating budgets of museums that comes from private giving is from the Museum Program Survey conducted in 1979 by the National Center for Education Statistics for the Institute of Museum Services.

For more information about the charitable deduction tax laws, see the Report of the Commission on Private Philanthropy and Public Needs, John H. Filer, chairman, *Giving in America: Toward a Stronger Voluntary Sector* (1975).

Page 114: Information about state support for the arts is from a fact sheet prepared by the National Assembly of State Arts Agencies (1984).

Page 114: Up-to-date information on support for museums is regularly reported in "Washington Report," a column in *Aviso*, the monthly newsletter of the American Association of Museums.

Page 114: The Museums Collaborative, Inc., survey is described by Susan Bertram in "Hard Times," *Museum News*, February 1983, pp. 20–25.

Page 115: Trends in private annual giving are described and statistically analyzed in the American Association of Fund-Raising Counsel's annual report, *Giving USA: 1984* (New York, 1984). The Business Committee for the Arts conducts an annual survey of corporate support of cultural institutions. For more information, write to Business Committee for the Arts, 1501 Broadway, New York, N.Y. 10036.

For more information about private sources of support for museums, see *Corporate Philanthropy* (Washington, D.C.: Council on Foundations, 1982); James C. Crimmins and Mary Keil, *Enterprise in the Nonprofit Sector* (Washington, D.C.: Partners for Livable Places, and New York: Rockefeller Brothers Fund, 1983); *Guide to Corporate Giving in the Arts* (New York: American Council for the Arts, 1983). From the Foundation Center in Washington, D.C., see *Grants for Museums* (1984), *Grants for Arts and Cultural Programs* (1984), and *The Foundation Index*, 13th ed. (1984).

Page 115: Information about the Keystone Awards and copies of *Corporate Social Responsibility: "Minnesota Strategies"* are available from the Greater Minneapolis Chamber of Commerce, Chamber of Commerce Building, 15 S. Fifth St., Minneapolis, Minn. 55402.

Page 116: Specific information about the organization and accomplishments of COMPAS are available from the COMPAS office, 1407 N. First St., Suite 1, Phoenix, Ariz. 85004. Similar fund-raising programs include COMBO in San Diego, California, and PONCHO in Seattle, Washington.

Appendix A: The Commission Process

Commission Meetings

January 11–13, 1982
Belmont Conference Center
Elkridge, Md.

June 20, 1982
Franklin Institute Science Museum
Philadelphia, Pa.

September 9–13, 1983
Scanticon-Princeton Conference Center
Princeton, N.J.

April 23, 1984
American Institute of Architects
Washington, D.C.

At its first meeting, the commission discussed issues of importance to the future of museums and outlined the nature and scope of its task. In Philadelphia, the commission planned the activities it would sponsor to acquire information about future trends and museum needs—open forums, colloquiums, a national monitoring system, involvement with the museum profession and staff research. In September 1983, commission members reviewed the information gathered through all its activities, discussed the content of the final report and drafted recommendations. At its final meeting, the commission reviewed the manuscript of the report.

Open Forums

The Museum and Community Identity
April 24, 1982
Louisiana State Museum
New Orleans, La.

The Diversity of Museum Audiences
November 15–16, 1982
California Palace of the Legion of Honor
San Francisco, Calif.

The Form and Function of Museum Spaces
December 6–7, 1982
Field Museum of Natural History
Chicago, Ill.

At open forums commission members met with invited participants to learn about the issues that define a museum's relationship to its community. Participants ranged from a group of eighth-grade students in New Orleans, to a leading state legislator in San Francisco, to a local television personality in Chicago. They were joined by an audience of 100 to 150 museum professionals, volunteers, trustees and interested members of the general public.

The commission covered substantial ground at the three forums. In New Orleans commission members joined civic leaders to talk about the museum's role in the development of a community's identity. In San Francisco participants considered a museum's new relationship to its diverse audience, a subject appropriate to a state experiencing rapid demographic changes. In Chicago, a city of architectural diversity, commission members heard from architects, critics and others about the form and function of museum spaces, alternative museum spaces for the future and the complex issue of intellectual access to what museums offer.

Colloquiums

Research in the Museum
November 22, 1982
National Museum of Natural History
Smithsonian Institution
Washington, D.C.
Richard Fiske, chairman

The Museum as an Educational Institution
December 17, 1982
Clark, Phipps, Clark & Harris, Inc.
New York, N.Y.
Mamie Phipps Clark, chairman

The Museum in Society
January 10, 1983
Museum of the City of New York
New York, N.Y.
Harold K. Skramstad, Jr., chairman

Collecting and Caring for Our Cultural and Natural
  Heritage
January 12, 1983
Missouri Botanical Garden
St. Louis, Mo.
Peter H. Raven, chairman

The colloquiums were designed as small, informal forums for frank discussions among commission members and invited experts. At each one eight to 12 people—museum leaders and outside experts—gathered for a daylong discussion of issues related to the colloquium topic.

At these sessions commission members heard many ideas and specific recommendations. Some common themes emerged from all the meetings. Outside experts urged the commission to lead the profession in developing a strong statement about the role of the museum as a social and educational institution. They helped commission members identify opportunities for museums in the future and encouraged the use of new technologies, the development of collaborative efforts and a renewed dedication to fundamental museum functions and responsibilities.

Involvement with the Museum Profession

From all corners of the museum community, through meetings, interviews, informal conversations and correspondence, the commission heard about the profession's hopes and concerns for the future. These ranged from questions about sensible limits of growth to anxiety about competing with the entertainment industry for visitors' leisure time. Commission members and staff attended meetings of state, regional and national museum associations, often speaking about the commission or participating in panel discussions.

Staff Research

The commission staff wrote position papers, prepared briefing materials and assembled lists of recommended readings designed to inform commission members and participants in the open forums and colloquiums about issues related to the future of America's museums. A complete set of these materials is on file at the American Association of Museums, 1055 Thomas Jefferson St., NW, Washington, D.C. 20007.

National Monitoring System

To acquire information about trends in museums, the commission established a pilot research project called the National Monitoring System. Sixty-two museums, selected through a stratified random sampling procedure, participated.

Data were collected with the help of a monitor in each museum who gathered information and presented it by telephone or mail to an interviewer at the commission office. The study design allowed for gathering survey data (attendance, sources of income, use of space), case study data (how specific museums are responding to economic conditions), attitudinal information (what the most important functions of the museum are considered to be) and thoughts about the future of museums.

Monitoring began in November 1982 and continued through October 1983. Information obtained from the study was used by the commission in its final report.

George H. J. Abrams is director, curator of ethnology and curator of history at the Seneca-Iroquois National Museum in Salamanca, New York. He was the founding chairman of the North American Indian Association and now serves on the board of the American Indian Development, Inc., and of the Museum of the American Indian in New York City. He also serves on professional committees, including those sponsored by the New York State Council on the Arts and the Smithsonian Institution, Washington, D.C.

Craig C. Black is director of the Natural History Museum of Los Angeles County and presidential appointee to the National Museum Services Board. He was president of the American Association of Museums from 1980 to 1982. He has served as president of the Society of Vertebrate Paleontology and the Association of Science Museum Directors and as chairman of the Museum Advisory Panel of the National Endowment for the Arts. From 1975 to 1982 he was director of the Carnegie Museum of Natural History, Carnegie Institute, Pittsburgh.

Joel N. Bloom is director of the Franklin Institute Science Museum and Planetarium in Philadelphia and cochairman of the Commission on Museums for a New Century. He is a former vice-president of the American Association of Museums and has served on the AAM Legislative Committee and Accreditation Commission. He is currently president of the Association of Science-Technology Centers and the Greater Philadelphia Cultural Alliance. He is also a commissioner of the U.S. National Commission for UNESCO and was a member of the Advisory Committee on Science Education of the National Science Foundation.

Mamie Phipps Clark (deceased August 11, 1983) was president of Museums Collaborative, Inc., and executive director of the Northside Center for Child Development in New York City. She served on the board of directors of the New York Public Library and the American Broadcasting Companies and was a member of the National Museum Services Board.

Mildred S. Compton is director emeritus of the Children's Museum of Indianapolis. She has served as president of the American Association of Youth Museums, the Midwest Museums Conference and the Association of Indiana Museums and as vice-president of the American Association of Museums. From 1976 to 1982 she was chairman of the AAM Accreditation Commission. She has also been a member of the executive board of the International Council of Museums Committee of the AAM.

William G. Conway is general director of the New York Zoological Society, which includes the Zoological Park (Bronx Zoo), the New York Aquarium, the Animal Research and Conservation Center and the Osborn Laboratories of Marine Sciences. He is a past president of the American Association of Zoological Parks and Aquariums. He has also been active as a trustee of the National Audubon Society, World Wildlife Fund–U.S., American Conservation Association, the International Council for Bird Preservation and the International Union for the Conservation of Nature and Natural Resources.

George Ewing is former cultural affairs officer of the state of New Mexico and director of the Museum of New Mexico in Santa Fe. He serves on the board of the Historic Santa Fe Foundation and is a member of the American Association of Anthropology and the American Association of Physical Anthropology.

Richard Fiske is director of the National Museum of Natural History and National Museum of Man at the Smithsonian Institution, Washington, D.C. He was a geologist in the museum's Department of Mineral Sciences and chief of the Office of Geochemistry and Geophysics, U.S. Geological Survey. He is a member of the Geological Society of America, the American Geophysical Union and the Geological Society of Washington, D.C.

Edmund Barry Gaither is director of the Museum of the National Center of Afro-American Artists and special consultant to the Museum of Fine Arts, Boston. He was cofounder and first president of the African-American Museums Association. He has taught art history at Wellesley College, Harvard University and Boston University. His work nationally and internationally has been in the interest of black artists and black professional visual arts institutions.

Nancy Hanks (deceased January 7, 1983) was chairman of the National Endowment for the Arts from 1969 to 1977 and president of the American Council for the Arts from 1967 to 1969. She also served as vice-president of the Rockefeller Brothers Fund, trustee of Duke University and director of the Equitable Life Assurance Society of the United States, Scholastic, Inc., and numerous non-profit organizations.

F. Wayne King is director of the Florida State Museum at the University of Florida in Gainesville. He has served as director of zoology and conservation at the New York Zoological Society and chairman of its education programs. He is a member of the American Association of Zoological Parks and Aquariums and served as chairman of its Wildlife and Conservation Committee. He has also served on the executive board of the American Committee for International Conservation and is the deputy chairman of the Species Survival Commission of the International Union for the Conservation of Nature and Natural Resources. He is treasurer of the Association of Systematics Collections.

Thomas W. Leavitt is director of the Herbert F. Johnson Museum of Art, Cornell University, Ithaca, New York, and president of the American Association of Museums. He was the first director of the Museum Program at the National Endowment for the Arts and has been director of the Santa Barbara Museum of Art and the Pasadena Art Museum. He is a former president of the Association of Art Museum Directors.

Richard W. Lyman is president of the Rockefeller Foundation in New York City and president emeritus of Stanford University. He was chairman of the Commission on the Humanities and a member and former vice-chairman of the National Council on the Humanities. He currently serves on the board of the Council on Foundations and is chairman of Independent Sector. He is also a director of IBM Corporation and of the Chase Manhattan Bank.

Robert R. Macdonald is director of the Louisiana State Museum, New Orleans. He is a vice-president of the American Association of Museums and has served on the AAM Council since 1979. He was executive director of the New Haven Colony Historical Society in Connecticut and director and curator of the Mercer Museum, Bucks County Historical Society, Doylestown, Pennsylvania.

Jan Keene Muhlert is director of the Amon Carter Museum of Art in Fort Worth, Texas. A trustee of the Association of Art Museum Directors and the American Arts Alliance, she also served on the Advisory Council of the National Museum Act. She has been director of the University of Iowa Museum of Art in Iowa City and associate curator of 20th-century painting and sculpture at the National Museum of American Art, Smithsonian Institution, Washington, D.C.

Franklin D. Murphy is chairman of the Executive Committee of the Times-Mirror Company of Los Angeles. He is a trustee of the National Gallery of Art, the Los Angeles County Museum of Art and the J. Paul Getty Museum. A former professor of medicine, he was chancellor of the University of Kansas, Lawrence, and the University of California at Los Angeles. He is also president of the Samuel H. Kress Foundation.

Helmuth J. Naumer is executive director of the San Antonio Museum Association. He has served as executive director of the Pacific Science Center in Seattle and the Fort Worth Museum of Science and History and was director of the Charlotte Nature Museum in North Carolina. He is a member of the AAM Council and a former trustee of the Art Museum Association. He has served on the Museum Advisory Panel of the National Endowment for the Arts and on the Museum Programs Advisory Committee of the National Endowment for the Humanities.

Richard E. Oldenburg is director of the Museum of Modern Art in New York City. He is a former chairman of the Museum Advisory Panel of the National Endowment for the Arts and has served on the Museum Aid Panel and Arts Programming for Television Panel of the New York State Council on the Arts. He is a member of the National Board of Consultants of the National Endowment for the Humanities.

Eldridge H. Pendleton is director of collections and programs at the Old York Historical Society, York, Maine. He has served as director of the Old Gaol Museum, also in York, and as curatorial assistant at Old Sturbridge Village in Massachusetts. He was an instructor of history at Princeton University and associate professor of American history at Sangamon State University in Springfield, Illinois. He was a member of the Museums/Conservation Panel of the Maine Commission on the Arts and Humanities, serves on the Advisory Committee of the Northeast Document Conservation Center and is cochairman of the Small Museums Committee of the New England Museum Association.

Earl A. Powell III is director of the Los Angeles County Museum of Art and cochairman of the Commission on Museums for a New Century. He was executive curator at the National Gallery of Art, Washington, D.C., and curator of the James Michener Collection at the University of Texas in Austin. He was also a teaching fellow in fine arts at Harvard University. He now serves on the board of directors of the American Arts Alliance and on the board of trustees of the American Federation of Arts.

Peter H. Raven is director of the Missouri Botanical Garden and professor of botany at Washington University in St. Louis. He is president of the American Institute of Biological Sciences, a past president of the Association of Systematics Collections and a member of the council of the National Academy of Sciences, the governing board of the National Research Council and the National Museum Services Board. He is also chairman of the National Science Foundation Advisory Committee on Biological, Behavioral and Social Sciences and a member of the Committee for Research and Exploration of the National Geographic Society.

Harold K. Skramstad, Jr., is president of the Edison Institute at Henry Ford Museum and Greenfield Village, Dearborn, Michigan. He has served as a member of the AAM Legislative Committee, Accreditation Commission and Council. He was director of the Chicago Historical Society and was chief of exhibit programs at the National Museum of American History, Smithsonian Institution, Washington, D.C. He currently serves as a trustee of the Center for Creative Studies in Detroit and is a director of the Detroit Symphony Orchestra.

Kenneth Starr is director of the Milwaukee Public Museum. He was president of the American Association of Museums from 1978 to 1980 and has also served as president of the Midwest Museums Conference and the Association of Science Museum Directors. He chaired the Drafting Committee of the Commission on Museums for a New Century and serves on the AAM Accreditation Commission. Formerly on the Advisory Council of the National Museum Act and the Museum Policy Panel of the National Endowment for the Arts, he is now on the NEA Conservation/Collections Management Panel and the Eleutherian Mills–Hagley (Museum) Foundation Advisory Committee.

William G. Swartchild, Jr. (deceased March 15, 1984) was a trustee and former chairman of the board of the Field Museum of Natural History in Chicago. He was also chairman of the board of the McGaw Medical Center, Northwestern University, and of the board of Children's Memorial Hospital and director of the Chicago Zoological Society (Brookfield Zoo). He was an active member of the AAM Trustee Committee and Committee on Ethics.

The commission consulted many people within and outside the museum community during the course of its work. Some of the following people were involved as participants or served on planning committees for the open forums; some attended colloquiums or served on panels at professional meetings. Others were consulted by staff or commission members in their research.

Cliff Abrams, Exhibit Designer
Field Museum of Natural History
Chicago, Ill.

Mary Alexander, Special Assistant to the Assistant Archivist
Public Programs and Exhibits, National Archives, Washington, D.C.

Kathy Arnaudin, Teacher
McMann School
New Orleans, La.

Nellie Arnold, Consultant
Arts and Culture State of California, Department of Parks and Recreation
Sacramento, Calif.

Malcolm Arth, Chairman and Curator of Education
American Museum of Natural History
New York, N.Y.

Susan Badder, Director of Education
Baltimore Museum of Art
Baltimore, Md.

Victor Banks, Designer
Vic Banks Productions
Chicago, Ill.

Joel A. Barker, President
Infinity Limited, Inc.
West St. Paul, Minn.

Mary Beachum, Librarian
Sara Tower Regional Library
Rome, Ga.

Arthur Beale, Director
Center for Conservation and Technical Studies, Fogg Art Museum, Harvard University
Cambridge, Mass.

Bruce Beasley, Artist
Oakland, Calif.

Gerard A. Bertrand, President
Massachusetts Audubon Society
Lincoln, Mass.

Carolyn Blackmon, Chairman
Department of Education, Field Museum of Natural History
Chicago, Ill.

Lindy Boggs
U.S. House of Representatives (D-Louisiana)
Washington, D.C.

Elizabeth M. Bolton, Preservation Leader
Alexandria, La.

Willard Boyd, President
Field Museum of Natural History
Chicago, Ill.

Steven L. Brezzo, Director
San Diego Museum of Art
San Diego, Calif.

R. Gary Bridge, Professor and Evaluator
Teachers College, Columbia University
New York, N.Y.

Ellsworth Brown, Director
Chicago Historical Society
Chicago, Ill.

Susan Brown, Staff Attorney
Mexican-American Legal Defense and Education Fund
San Francisco, Calif.

Tamra Carboni, Curator of Education
Louisiana State Museum
New Orleans, La.

Charles Carmichael, President
Godwin Advertising Agency
Jackson, Miss.

Cary Carson, Director of Research
Colonial Williamsburg
Williamsburg, Va.

E. Laurence Chalmers, Jr., President
Art Institute of Chicago
Chicago, Ill.

Patricia Chandler, Arts Coordinator and Curator
Katz and Besthoff Corporation
New Orleans, La.

Albert Cheng, Coordinator of Bilingual Education
San Francisco Unified School District
San Francisco, Calif.

Timothy Chester, Chief Curator and Decorative Arts Curator
Louisiana State Museum
New Orleans, La.

Merrilee Clark, Public Information Officer
Chicago Park District
Chicago, Ill.

Joseph F. Coates, President
J. F. Coates, Inc.
Washington, D.C.

T. Allan Comp, Chief
Division of Cultural Resources, National Park Service,
    Pacific Northwest Region
Seattle, Wash.

Sally Cornish, Programs Coordinator
World Future Society
Bethesda, Md.

M. J. Czarniecki III, Director
Minnesota Museum of Art
St. Paul, Minn.

James J. Deetz, Director
Robert H. Lowie Museum of Anthropology, University
    of California
Berkeley, Calif.

Mike Demetrion, President
Marine World–Africa USA
Redwood City, Calif.

Janice Driesbach, Exhibit Coordinator
Oakland Museum
Oakland, Calif.

Gregg Edwards, Program Manager
National Science Foundation
Washington, D.C.

Stephen Edwards, Executive Director
Association of Systematics Collections, Museum of
    Natural History, University of Kansas
Lawrence, Kans.

Charles Eldredge, Director
National Museum of American Art
Washington, D.C.

Gary Esolen, Editor
Gambit Publications
New Orleans, La.

Julian Euell, Director
Oakland Museum
Oakland, Calif.

Gregory Farmer, Director
Connecticut Valley Historical Museum
Springfield, Mass.

Victor Ferkiss, Professor of Government
Georgetown University
Washington, D.C.

William Ferris, Director
Center for the Study of Southern Culture, University of
    Mississippi
University, Miss.

Roger Field, Science and Health Reporter
WBBM-TV
Chicago, Ill.

Carol Fields, Writer
San Francisco, Calif.

John Fowler, Director of Special Projects
National Science Teachers Association
Washington, D.C.

Diane B. Frankel, Director
Center for Museum Studies, John F. Kennedy
    University
San Francisco, Calif.

L. Thomas Frye, Curator
Oakland Museum
Oakland, Calif.

Melinda Young Frye, Consultant
Alexandria, Va.

Paul Gapp, Architecture Critic
Chicago Tribune
Chicago, Ill.

Jane Glaser, Program Manager
Office of Museum Programs, Smithsonian Institution
Washington, D.C.

Jerome Clayton Glenn, Executive Director
Partnership for Productivity
Washington, D.C.

Sheila Grinnell, Consultant
Oakland, N.J.

W. L. Hadley Griffin, Chairman of the Board
Brown Group
St. Louis, Mo.

Christine Hansen, Demographer
U.S. Census Bureau
Washington, D.C.

Neil Harris, Professor of History
University of Chicago
Chicago, Ill.

J. Edwin Hendricks, Professor of History
Wake Forest University
Winston-Salem, N.C.

Linda Hermesman, Aide
Montgomery County Council
Rockville, Md.

Katharine Holland, Director of Research/Collections/
    Registration
San Francisco Museum of Modern Art
San Francisco, Calif.

Adrienne Horn, Administrator for Professional
    Development
Center for Museum Studies, John F. Kennedy
    University
San Francisco, Calif.

Harold Horowitz, Director of Research
National Endowment for the Arts
Washington, D.C.

Barbara Marx Hubbard, Director
Campaign for a Positive Future
Palo Alto, Calif.

Edward Hudlin, Chairman
Institute for Humanistic Studies
Edwardsville, Ill.

Peggy Hunt, Teacher
Baton Rouge, La.

Perry Huston, Conservator
Kimbell Art Museum
Fort Worth, Tex.

Robert Hutchins, Architect
Skidmore, Owings and Merrill
Chicago, Ill.

Carole Huxley, Deputy Commissioner for Cultural
    Education
New York State Department of Education
Albany, N.Y.

Alan Jacobs, Chairman
Department of City and Regional Planning, University
    of California
Berkeley, Calif.

Ruth Jacobson, Advertising Executive
Fleishman-Hillard, Inc.
St. Louis, Mo.

John Jones, Supervisor of Social Studies
New Orleans Public Schools
New Orleans, La.

Lynn Jorgensen, Director
Art Museum Association
San Francisco, Calif.

Paul Joslin, Assistant Director
Brookfield Zoo
Brookfield, Ill.

Lawrence Kaagan, Vice-President and Assistant to the
    Chairman
Yankelovich, Skelly and White
New York, N.Y.

David Kennedy, Superintendent of Science and
    Environmental Education
Washington State Public School System
Olympia, Wash.

Alan Knox, Professor of Education
University of Wisconsin
Madison, Wis.

Donald LaBadie, Art and Architecture Critic
Commerical Appeal
Memphis, Tenn.

W. M. Laetsch, Vice-Chancellor for Undergraduate
    Affairs
University of California
Berkeley, Calif.

Linda Liebes, Director
Coyote Point Museum for Environmental Education
San Mateo, Calif.

Lucy Lim, Executive Director
Chinese Culture Center of San Francisco
San Francisco, Calif.

Gordon L. Lippitt, Professor of Behavioral Science
Department of Psychiatry and Behavioral Science,
    George Washington University
Washington, D.C.

Dennis Little, Director
Merit Systems Review and Studies, Merit Systems
    Protection Board
Washington, D.C.

Jean Ludlow, Manager of Public Relations and
    Advertising
Prudential Insurance Company
Jacksonville, Fla.

Paula March, Registrar for Exhibitions
Fine Arts Museums of San Francisco
San Francisco, Calif.

Peter C. Marzio, Director
Museum of Fine Arts
Houston, Tex.

Roy Mason, Architect
Roy Mason Architects
Washington, D.C.

James F. Mello, Associate Director
National Museum of Natural History
Washington, D.C.

Arthur Mielke, Public Information Specialist
U.S. Census Bureau
Washington, D.C.

Henry A. Millon, Dean
Center for Advanced Study in the Visual Arts, National
    Gallery of Art
Washington, D.C.

Ernest Mittelberger (deceased), Director
Wine Museum of San Francisco
San Francisco, Calif.

Sybil Morial, Community Leader
New Orleans, La.

Marena Grant Morrisey, Executive Director
Loch Haven Art Center
Orlando, Fla.

Rex Moser, Executive Director
Museum Education, Art Institute of Chicago
Chicago, Ill.

Richard C. Muhlberger, Director
George Walter Vincent Smith Art Museum and
    Museum of Fine Arts
Springfield, Mass.

Alma Neal, Docent
Beauregard Keyes House
New Orleans, La.

John H. Neff, Art Advisor
First National Bank of Chicago
Chicago, Ill.

Lorin I. Nevling, Jr., Director
Field Museum of Natural History
Chicago, Ill.

Joseph Veach Noble, Director
Museum of the City of New York
New York, N.Y.

Gustav A. Noren, General Services Administrator
Field Museum of Natural History
Chicago, Ill.

Jay Ogilvie, Researcher
Stanford Research Institute
Menlo Park, Calif.

Frank Oppenheimer, Director
Exploratorium
San Francisco, Calif.

Thomas Palumbo, Supervisory Survey Statistician
U.S. Census Bureau
Washington, D.C.

Arva Moore Parks, Historian
Coral Gables, Fla.

William Pattison, Professor of Education
University of Chicago
Chicago, Ill.

Paul N. Perrot, Director
Virginia Museum of Fine Arts
Richmond, Va.

Edmund Pillsbury, Director
Kimbell Art Museum
Fort Worth, Tex.

Bonnie Pitman-Gelles, Associate Director
Public Programs, Seattle Art Museum
Seattle, Wash.

Gaines Post, Jr., Professor of History
University of Texas
Austin, Tex.

George Rabb, Director
Brookfield Zoo
Brookfield, Ill.

Danielle Rice, Curator of Education
National Gallery of Art
Washington, D.C.

Leon Richelle, Chancellor
University of New Orleans
New Orleans, La.

Paul E. Rivard, Director
Maine State Museum
Augusta, Maine

Peter Rodriquez, Executive Director
Mexican Museum
San Francisco, Calif.

Jerome G. Rozen, Jr., Deputy Director for Research
American Museum of Natural History
New York, N.Y.

Virginia Rubin, Executive Associate
Exploratorium
San Francisco, Calif.

Viki Sand, Director
Shaker Museum
Old Chatham, N.Y.

Chiz Schultz, Executive Producer
Children's Television Workshop
New York, N.Y.

Franz Schulze, Professor of Art History
Lake Forest College
Highland Park, Ill.

Catherine Scott, Librarian
Museum Reference Center, Smithsonian Institution
Washington, D.C.

Monica Scott, Executive Director
San Francisco African American Historical Society and
    Cultural Society
San Francisco, Calif.

Robert Semper, Associate Director
Exploratorium
San Francisco, Calif.

John Settle, Attorney
Settle and Nesbitt
Shreveport, La.

Mary Beth Shank, Librarian
Center for Coordination of Research on Social
    Indicators
Washington, D.C.

Catherine Shumate, Assistant Editor
Chicago Reader
Chicago, Ill.

Sybil Simmon, Director
Arts and Business Council of New York
New York, N.Y.

Janet Smith, Director, Department of Programs
Chicago Council on Fine Arts
Chicago, Ill.

Norris K. Smith, Professor of Art History
Washington University
St. Louis, Mo.

David Pearce Snyder, Futurist
Snyder Family Enterprise
Bethesda, Md.

Michael Spock, Director
Children's Museum
Boston, Mass.

I. Ezra Staples, Executive Director
Area Council for Economic Education
Philadelphia, Pa.

Kevin Starr, Columnist
San Francisco Examiner
San Francisco, Calif.

Tedwilliam Theodore, President
Center for New Television
Chicago, Ill.

Lawrence W. Towner, Director
Newberry Library
Chicago, Ill.

George Tressel, Program Director
Scientific and Engineering Personnel and Education,
   National Science Foundation
Washington, D.C.

James Tyler, Program Director
Biological Research Resources Program, National
   Science Foundation
Washington, D.C.

Christina Valaitis, Program Officer
Illinois Humanities Council
Champaign, Ill.

Alene Valkanos, Cultural and Public Affairs
   Coordinator
Chicago World's Fair—1992 Authority
Chicago, Ill.

John Vasconcellos, California State Assemblyman
Twenty-third District
Sacramento, Calif.

Carl Warachowski, Former Aquarist
John G. Shedd Aquarium
Chicago, Ill.

Brooke H. Warrick, Senior Consultant
Values and Lifestyles Program, SRI International
Menlo Park, Calif.

Katharine Watson, Director
Bowdoin College Museum of Art
Brunswick, Maine

Harry Weese, Architect
Harry Weese Associates
Chicago, Ill.

Phoebe Weil, Chief Conservator
Center for Archeometry, Washington University
St. Louis, Mo.

Stephen E. Weil, Deputy Director
Hirshhorn Museum and Sculpture Garden,
   Smithsonian Institution
Washington, D.C.

Rudolph H. Weingartner, Dean
College of Arts and Sciences, Northwestern University
Evanston, Ill.

Judith Weisman, Head of Education and Public
   Programs
Chicago Historical Society
Chicago, Ill.

Morton Weisman, Executive Director
Chicago Architecture Foundation
Chicago, Ill.

Mary Jane White, Former Director
TAP Program, American Council of Life Insurance
Washington, D.C.

Townsend Wolfe III, Executive Director
Arkansas Arts Center
Little Rock, Ark.

Jackie Woods, Executive Director
New Muse Community Museum of Brooklyn
Brooklyn, N.Y.

In addition to the commission staff, other AAM staff
members, consultants and volunteers contributed to the
work of the commission and the publication of this
report. They are Gail Anderson, Nancy Brockman,
Carol A. Constantine, Tracey Linton Craig, Linda
Currie, Gloria Feeney, Patricia W. Fisher, Mary Lou
Hansen, Maureen Robinson, Tracy Soulges, Leslie
van der Lee and Laurie E. Wertz.

These institutions, a representative sample of American museums by size, type and geographic location, participated in the commission's National Monitoring System, a pilot research project designed to gather information about trends in museums.

Adler Planetarium
Chicago, Ill.

Albright-Knox Art Gallery
Buffalo, N.Y.

Arms Museum
Youngstown, Ohio

Arnold Arboretum
Jamaica Plain, Mass.

Brooklyn Historical Society Museum
Brooklyn, N.Y.

Buffalo Bill Historical Center
Cody, Wyo.

Butler Institute of American Art
Youngstown, Ohio

California Museum of Afro-American History and
   Culture
Los Angeles, Calif.

California Museum of Science and Industry
Los Angeles, Calif.

Carnegie Museum of Natural History
Pittsburgh, Pa.

Central Arizona Museum of History
Phoenix, Ariz.

Children's Museum
Boston, Mass.

Clayville Rural Life Center Museum
Springfield, Ill.

Columbus Museum of Arts and Science
Columbus, Ga.

Columbus Zoo
Powell, Ohio

Daughters of the American Revolution Museum
Washington, D.C.

Evanston Historical Society
Evanston, Ill.

Fairfield Historical Society
Fairfield, Conn.

Field Museum of Natural History
Chicago, Ill.

Florida State Museum
Gainesville, Fla.

Fort Bliss Replica Museum
Fort Bliss, Tex.

Fort Worth Museum of Science
Fort Worth, Tex.

Gore Place Society
Waltham, Mass.

Grove Farm Homestead
Lihue, Hawaii

Gunston Hall Plantation
Lorton, Va.

Hall of Science of the City of New York
Flushing, N.Y.

Hammond Castle Museum
Gloucester, Mass.

Heard Natural Science Museum
McKinney, Tex.

Hermitage
Ho-Ho Kus, N.J.

High Point Historical Society
High Point, N.C.

James Buchanan Museum
Lancaster, Pa.

Joslyn Art Museum
Omaha, Nebr.

Kansas Health Museum
Halstead, Kans.

Lawrence Hall of Science, University of California
Berkeley, Calif.

Louis E. May Museum
Fremont, Nebr.

Maxwell Museum of Anthropology, University of New
   Mexico
Albuquerque, N. Mex.

McKinley Museum of History, Science & Industry
Canton, Ohio

Michigan Historical Museum
Lansing, Mich.

Morris County Historical Society—Acorn Hall
Morristown, N.J.

Munson-Williams-Proctor Institute
Utica, N.Y.

Museum of Indian Heritage, Eagle Creek Park
Indianapolis, Ind.

Museum of the Rockies, Montana State University
Bozeman, Mont.

Natural Science Center of Greensboro
Greensboro, N.C.

Naval War College Museum
Newport, R.I.

Newark Museum
Newark, N.J.

New Orleans Museum of Art
New Orleans, La.

Northern Indiana Historical Society
South Bend, Ind.

Old Jail Foundation
Albany, Tex.

Palm Springs Desert Museum
Palm Springs, Calif.

Please Touch Museum
Philadelphia, Pa.

Polk Public Museum at Lakeland
Lakeland, Fla.

Potsdam Public Museum
Potsdam, N.Y.

Rice Museum
Georgetown, S.C.

San Diego Museum of Man
San Diego, Calif.

Santa Barbara Museum of Art
Santa Barbara, Calif.

Science Museum
Springfield, Mass.

Southeast Arkansas Arts and Science Center
Pine Bluff, Ark.

Utah State Historical Society
Salt Lake City, Utah

Virginia Military Institute Museum
Lexington, Va.

Virginia Museum of Fine Arts
Richmond, Va.

Wellesley College Museum, Jewett Arts Center
Wellesley, Mass.

William Clark Market House Museum
Paducah, Ky.

Photo Credits

16, 88: Baltimore Museum of Art, Alex Castro; 19, 54: Smithsonian Institution; 20, 34, 40: Los Angeles County Museum of Natural History; 22: National Gallery of Art, Chip Clark; 26, 27: Computer Museum; 29: Solomon R. Guggenheim Museum, Robert E. Mates; 39, 84: New York Botanical Garden, Allen Rokach; 43, 48: Toledo Museum of Art; 44: Metropolitan Museum of Art, Henry Groskinsky; 45: High Museum of Art, Ezra Stoller/ESTO; 46: George Eastman House; 49: Yale Center for British Art, Michael Marsland; 51: Lowie Museum of Anthropology, University of California, Berkeley; 56: Dan Danilowicz; 58: Franklin Institute Science Museum; 60: Norwegian-American Museum; 61: Everson Museum of Art, Ezra Stoller/ESTO; 63: Corcoran Gallery of Art, Joel Breger; 64: Whitney Museum of American Art, Carol Halebian; 66: Boston Children's Museum, Richard Howard; 68: Brookfield Zoo; 72: Louisville Museum of Natural History and Science, Michael Webb, Ray Schulmann, Caulfield & Shook; 75: Museum of Fine Arts, Boston; 77: Baltimore Museum of Art, Arnold Kramer; 80: National Aquarium, Norman McGrath; 81, 108: Kimbell Art Museum, Bob Wharton; 82: Harry Hartman; 92: Guthrie Theater, Bruce Goldstein; 96: Yale University, Sven Martson; 97: Littleton Historical Museum; 98: Brooks Memorial Art Gallery; 101: Yale University, T. Charles Erickson; 102: Studio Museum in Harlem, Frank Stewart; 106: Milwaukee Art Museum, Dale Guldan; 107: Herbert F. Johnson Museum of Art, Nathaniel Lieberman; 111: Frick Collection; 112: Franklin Institute Science Museum, I. George Bilyk; 113: Rouse Company; 126: Walker Art Center.

Index

Museums for a New Century was designed by Alex and Caroline Castro, Hollowpress, Baltimore, Maryland.

The text was telecommunicated by the American Association of Museums and is set in Walbaum and 'Linotype' Walbaum processed by Monotype Composition Company, Baltimore, Maryland.

The book was printed on Consolidated Papers 80lb Paloma Coated Matte, by Garamond/Pridemark Press, Baltimore, Maryland. The cover is 10 point Appleton Silver/White Currency cover with silver foil stamping.